NURTURING PROGRAM
For Teenage Parents and Their Families

Parent Handbook

Stephen J. Bavolek and Juliana Dellinger-Bavolek

NP4-PHB

Family Development Resources, Inc.
3160 Pinebrook Road
Park City, UT 84060

Welcome Teenage Parents and Children

Welcome to the *Nurturing Program for Teenage Parents and Their Families*. We are very pleased that you have decided to learn about ways to nurture yourself and your children.

We are sure you will agree that being a teenager and a parent at the same time is not easy. With all the demands of adolescence facing you each day like dating, relationships, school, friends, expectations from your mother and father, being a mother or a father, in addition to all these other issues, is indeed challenging. That is why we are very pleased you are attending the Nurturing Program.

To nurture means to "take care of". When you nurture yourself, you do things that show others you care for yourself. When you nurture others, you demonstrate your ability and willingness to care for others. It is precisely what the Nurturing Program is all about: learning to nurture yourself and your children.

Activities in the Nurturing Program will help you become more aware of yourself as a teenager. You will be asked to share parts of yourself (past, present, and future) with others. You will examine and discuss issues teenagers have to constantly deal with like dating, sex, drugs, AIDS, friends, your future, your expectations, as well as your dreams, goals, and fantasies. It will be an exciting time for you to grow.

You will also learn how to become a more nurturing mother or father to your children. You will learn how to help your children grow up healthy with positive feelings and thoughts about themselves. You will learn how to use discipline, rewards and punishment in ways that promote a positive regard of self—not a negative one. Activities will help you learn what to expect and when to expect your children to do certain things; how to have fun with your children; and how to grow as a family.

All of these things can be achieved by you—but there is one catch. We need you to attend the sessions with your children and give it your all. We need your commitment to be a better person and a better parent. Like you, we want to be the best parents we can be to our sons. We would like to give them more and better than what we had as children. It's a common desire among all parents. Don't quit trying. When life appears to be really overwhelming—hang in there—get the support you need and keep going.

Mountains can be climbed and marathons can be run, but it takes conviction. We wish you and your children the absolute best in love, courage, and nurturing.

Stephen J. Bovelek
Juliana Dellinger-Bavolek

About the Authors

Stephen J. Bavolek, Ph.D., is a nationally recognized leader in the fields of parent education and prevention of child abuse and neglect. He has a professional background working with emotionally disturbed children and adolescents in schools and residential settings, and abused children and abusive parents in treatment programs. He completed a postdoctoral internship at the Kempe Center for the Prevention and Treatment of Child Abuse in Denver, Colorado, and was selected by Phi Delta Kappa as one of 75 young educators in the country who represent the best in educational leadership, research, and services. Dr. Bavolek has conducted extensive research in the prevention and treatment of child abuse and neglect and parent education. He is the author of *A Handbook for Understanding Child Abuse and Neglect,* a comprehensive examination of maltreatment to children, and *The Adult-Adolescent Parenting Inventory;* a valid measure designed to assess high risk parenting attitudes. In addition, Dr. Bavolek is the principal author of the *Nurturing Program for Parents and Children, 4 to 12 Years; Nurturing Program for Parents and Children Birth to 5 years*; and *Nurturing Program for Parents and Adolescents.*

Juliana Dellinger-Bavolek, M.S.E., is a parent-child training specialist. Ms. Bavolek's professional background includes intensive experience with preschool handicapped children and their families, both as a classroom teacher/home visitor and as a facilitator of support groups for parents of infants and toddlers with special needs. As a training specialist with the Portage Project Region V Head Start Training Center, Ms. Bavolek provided training and technical assistance to Head Start home visit staff in implementing services for culturally disadvantaged parents and their preschool children. Ms. Bavolek served as the Education/Handicap Services Coordinator for Head Start and Parent-Child Centers in a seven county area in Wisconsin. She continues to work as a consultant to special education programs in the public schools and to Head Start and Parent-Child Centers nationally.

A fire fly flitted by.
"Look," I said,
But I was alone.

Author Unknown

This book is dedicated to the thousands of teenage parents who are trying to be the best people and parents they can be.

This book is dedicated to you and your child.

Contents

Program Orientation

1. The Nurturing Program for Teenage Parents and Their Families consists of 20 group-based sessions or 40 home-based sessions.

2. Each group-based session lasts 2 1/2 hours. Each home-based session lasts 1 1/2 hours.

3. The format of each session is:

   a. **Icebreaker and Home Practice Check-In.** Each session will begin with an Icebreaker much like today's session began. The Icebreaker will be followed by a brief check-in time to see how you are doing and how successful you were in completing your home practice exercise. The Icebreaker and Home Practice Check-In will last 20 minutes.

   b. **Discussion.** After the Icebreaker and check-in time, we will discuss issues related to our role as parents, or issues that present themselves to adolescents. The focus will be on developing a nurturing self. The discussion will last 30 minutes for the home-based program and 50 minutes for the group-based program.

   c. **Family Nurturing Time.** Following the discussion will be the Family Nurturing Time where teen parents and their children will spend time together. Families will play, laugh, sing songs, and learn about positive touch. Snack and beverages will be served during this time. The Family Nurturing Time will last 30 minutes.

   d. **Discussion (Group-based Program Only).** We will again discuss issues related to our roles as parents, or issues that present themselves to adolescents. Focus will be on developing a nurturing self. This discussion will last 50 minutes.

   e. **Group/Family Hug.** Each session will end with a group/family hug. During the group hug, we can say anything positive and discuss the home practice exercise. Children are included in the group/family hug. The group/family hug will last 3 minutes.

The group/family hug is an important part of each session.

4. Each week, you will be responsible for trying your best to complete the home practice exercise. Sometimes it will involve writing a few things. Most of the time it involves practicing new skills.

5. A constant part of your weekly home practice exercise is to spend 30 minutes each day with your children in play/fun time. That means no TV. Reading books and practicing the new nurturing touch techniques are things you can do in the 30 minutes.

6. The *Parent Handbook* is a resource book and workbook that contains weekly information and exercises. Each teen parent should have his/her own copy and should bring it to each session.

7. There are seven nurturing booklets to be used as informational guides, activities manuals, and as a scrap book:

    a. *Memories and Developmental Milestones*

    b. *Infant Massage Manual*

    c. *Activities for Infants*

    d. *Activities for Toddlers*

    e. *Activities for Preschoolers*

    f. *Special Day Celebrations*

    g. *Flu Bug Blues*

8. The *Infant Massage Manual* will be used to help you and your children learn gentle touch, stress relaxation, and positive parent-child interactions. Each weekly home practice exercise will include activites from the *Infant Massage Manual*, *Activities Manuals for Infants*, *Activities Manual for Toddlers*, and *Activities Manual for Preschoolers*.

9. There are three inventories to complete at the beginning and end of the program. The purpose of these inventories is to see how much you have gained in knowledge and awareness. The results of the inventories will be reviewed and discussed with your facilitator.

10. General expectations for the program sessions:

    a. To be honest—good or bad.

    b. To do home practice exercises.

    c. To ask questions if a concept is not understood.

    d. To make a commitment to grow.

    e. To laugh and have a good time.

Be involved and have a good time.

Nurturing Program
for Teenage Parents and Their Families

Welcome to the Nurturing Program. As you probably already know, raising children is not an easy task. Being a parent requires dedication, sacrifice, skill, knowledge, love, and compassion. The hours are long, there are no paid vacations, and you must be on call 24 hours every day of the year to perform activities that range from changing diapers to comforting a frightened child. In our culture, the fascination toward becoming a mother or father is unequaled. At some time in their lives, almost all young girls and boys dream about the day that they will have children of their own. Surprisingly, the majority of us who do become parents do so with little or no formal training.

Learning to Become Parents

Did you ever wonder how we learn to become parents? For the most part, young men and women learn about raising children through various informal means. Let's review some of the popular beliefs.

An instinct is an inborn tendency to act in a certain manner. Some people believe that raising children is instinctual and that this ability is brought out when your first child is born. Supposedly, parents are then capable of providing the love, nurturing, skill, and compassion necessary to raise a healthy child.

Not everyone supports the instinctual theory of parenting. Many believe that parenting is a learned behavior that starts very early in our lives. The way we learn how to become parents is a process called modeling. Modeling means that as parents, we use the same techniques for raising our children that our parents used on us when we were kids.

The expressions "like father-like son" or "like mother-like daughter" suggest we will behave like our father or mother because of the many experiences we had with them. Our parents had certain thoughts about discipline, punishment, communication, chores, expectations, etc., which they practiced. Being brought up with their manner of parenting, we learned their techniques. Given similar situations, we will "model" their behaviors with our own children.

The experiences we had with our parents probably account for the greater part of our parenting training. There are also other factors which have influenced our style of child rearing. Influencing our parenting abilities are the environment we grew up in, our parent's financial status, the culture or subculture our family was a part of, our ethnic heritage, our race, our religious beliefs, our birth order, and whether we are male or female.

For some of us, the messages we received and the models we watched were mostly positive. These messages gave us a good start in parenting our children. Although there were bad times, the majority of interactions with mom and dad were positive. They left a good impression.

For a lot of us, however, the messages we received and the models we observed were frequently negative. These negative messages resulted in learning inappropriate parenting behaviors.

Harsh and abusive parents, experiences, and environments leave a distorted view of what the roles of a child and a parent are all about. Their impact is observed in the countless number of abusive acts committed each year on children, spouses, and the elderly.

Learning Appropriate Developmental Expectations

Our belief is that parenting is a learned behavior. Old undesirable patterns of interactions between parents and children can be replaced with new, more desirable ones. We built the parenting and nurturing program that you and your children will be a part of around this premise.

Part of our focus will be on increasing your knowledge of the developmental capabilities of children at various ages. Such knowledge will better prepare you to establish age-appropriate expectations for your children's behavior.

You will learn how and when children can accomplish certain tasks. You will also learn the physical, social, and emotional skills necessary to complete the tasks.

You will also become aware of the negative impact inappropriate expectations have upon a developing self-concept.

You will not be alone in learning these skills. Your children will be learning comparable skills. Activities in the children's program encourage the development of a positive self-concept by allowing children to master age-appropriate tasks.

Learning Appropriate Behavior Management Techniques

A major part of our focus will be on increasing your knowledge and ability to use appropriate behavior management techniques with your children. We base our training on the philosophy that hitting children for any reason is abusive. Alternatives to hitting will result in better adjusted children.

During the program, we will discuss and role play various appropriate ways of disciplining and punishing your children. These ways are immeasurably more effective than hitting. You will also learn how to reward children for who they are and the things they do.

Your children will also be learning the same forms of discipline and ways of being punished and rewarded. Our goal is to give you and your children experiences in appropriate types of discipline, rewards, and punishment.

Use appropriate behavior management techniques.

Increasing Self-Awareness

Raising healthy children takes more than having the right expectations, or knowing appropriate ways of disciplining, rewarding, and punishing your children. Parenting children is also a deeply emotional experience that requires you, the parent, to maintain an awareness of your own needs.

Not losing sight of your own social and emotional needs as a teenager will help you in maintaining an identity of yourself outside of your role as a parent. Becoming aware of and being able to find ways to meet your needs, is a major focus of our program.

Find appropriate ways to get your own needs met.

Activities will challenge you to understand who you are by identifying your personal strengths and weaknesses. Our experiences have told us that when teenagers become aware of themselves as individuals, they increase their ability to become healthy, loving, nurturing parents to their children.

In addition, your children will also be increasing their awareness of their own needs, feelings, strengths, weaknesses, likes, and dislikes. Art, music, communication, and play will accomplish this awareness. You and your children will be growing together through an awareness of your self needs.

Increasing Ability to be Empathic

In becoming a nurturing parent, you will use awareness of your feelings, strengths, weaknesses, likes, and dislikes to become more aware of these in your children. It forms the cornerstone of our program.

Being empathic means you will be able to help your children grow up as healthy, independent, caring, empathic individuals. What more could any child ever ask of his parents.

Your children will also be increasing their ability to become empathically aware of the needs of others. Activities will encourage children to share, play cooperatively, listen to the needs of others, and support a friend in time of need.

Learning new skills and knowledge is not always an easy task. With a sincere effort, you and your family can begin to enjoy more satisfying and caring interactions.

WELCOME TO OUR PROGRAM!

Skill Strips

Match the skill with the correct age period. Circle the age you think children should begin to perform the behavior.

Behaviors	0-12 months A	12-24 months B	24-36 months C	36-48 months D	48-60 months E
Takes a few steps without support	A	B	C	D	E
Repeats same syllable 2-3 times	A	B	C	D	E
Builds tower of 3 blocks	A	B	C	D	E
Says 5 different words	A	B	C	D	E
Points to 3 body parts on self	A	B	C	D	E
Uses pincer grasp to pick up object	A	B	C	D	E
Imitates peek-a-boo	A	B	C	D	E
Pulls off socks	A	B	C	D	E
Holds and drinks from cup using 2 hands	A	B	C	D	E
Follows rules by imitating actions of other children	A	B	C	D	E
Snaps or hooks clothing	A	B	C	D	E
Pedals tricycle 5 feet	A	B	C	D	E
Attempts to help parent with tasks by doing part of a chore (e.g. hold dust pan)	A	B	C	D	E
Walks backwards	A	B	C	D	E
Will attend for 5 minutes while a story is read	A	B	C	D	E
Sucks liquid from glass using a straw	A	B	C	D	E
Imitates counting to 3	A	B	C	D	E
Puts on mittens	A	B	C	D	E
Holds up fingers to tell age	A	B	C	D	E
Uses word for bathroom need	A	B	C	D	E
Stands on one foot for 4-8 seconds	A	B	C	D	E
Uses words: sister, brother, grandmother, grandfather	A	B	C	D	E
Stays dry all night	A	B	C	D	E
Takes turns with 8-9 other children	A	B	C	D	E
Draws a man (head, trunk, 4 limbs)	A	B	C	D	E
Engages in socially acceptable behavior in public	A	B	C	D	E

Ages and Stages: Development of Children

Developmental stages are periods of time children grow and learn new behaviors. At each stage, children are capable of doing only certain things because of their size, age, and maturity. The four general kinds of developmental stages are:

1. **Physical development** means that as children get older they usually get bigger. Usually when they get older and bigger, their gross motor and fine motor skills increase. Gross motor means activities like running, throwing, jumping, crawling, etc. Fine motor means activities like writing, holding a fork and knife, using scissors, etc. Physical development is important for helping children not only increase their skills but also organize their behaviors.

2. **Intellectual development** means that children learn more the older they get. They learn to recognize shapes and colors, recite the alphabet, figure out problems, and many other things. These intellectual abilities continue to increase as children continue to grow.

3. **Language development** means that as children grow older, their communication skills increase. Their ability to use words, phrases, and sentences in writing and in conversation help them gain mastery of their environment by expressing their needs and understanding the needs of others. Language expands from a few simple sounds during the first year of life to the use of thousands of words in their teen years.

4. **Social and emotional development** go hand-in-hand. The way we treat children and the care they receive affect the way they mature and are capable of interacting with others. Children's emotional growth goes from an early stage of dependence and taking to a later stage of independence and giving.

Everyone Goes Through Stages of Growth

All children go through developmental stages as they grow and mature into adults. In fact, developmental stages continue right into old age. We all go through stages, some of us faster than others, and some of us more thoroughly than others.

A word of caution. No child is "average" in all areas of growth. Children are unique. Some are better at doing certain tasks than others. The experiences and opportunities children have, as well as the abilities they are born with, influence their development.

No child is "average" in all areas of growth.

What Developmental Stages Tell Us

At different times in our lives, from infancy to adulthood, we are capable of doing certain things. Running, lifting heavy objects, talking, feeding ourselves, being able to care for someone else, are some of these capabilities. Developmental stages actually serve as rough guides for giving parents an idea when children may be capable of performing desired behaviors. These stages do not serve as the final word on children's abilities. Not all children are capable of performing a behavior just because a stage says they should. General knowledge of developmental stages gives parents a good idea what children may be capable of doing.

Children learn to do certain skills at different ages.

We learn about developmental stages because we want to become the best parents we can. We also learn about developmental stages because it makes the life of being an infant and a young child easier and happier. Being an infant is not always that pleasant. There are very few things infants can do by themselves besides sleep, cry, wet and soil themselves, and burp. They even have to learn to turn over once they are lying on their backs. It's not simple. Life gets easier as infants get older because they can do more things independently.

Imagine if parents didn't know what infants or children were capable of doing at different times in their lives. Childhood would be a frustrating experience. We might ask small infants to feed themselves. We might expect young children to set the table, cook the meals, or do the dishes. When we place such inappropriate expectations on children, the children can't complete the task, and they begin to feel bad about themselves.

Developmental Stages and Self-Concept

When we complete a task, no matter how large or small, we usually feel as if we accomplished something. People often notice our accomplishments and usually praise us for our efforts. The praise we receive helps build in us a positive feeling about ourselves or a positive self-concept. Trouble begins to occur when we constantly fail to accomplish something. No one recognizes our efforts and we don't receive any praise. In fact, we often receive just the opposite — criticism about how we can't do anything or how bad we are. When this happens often, we begin to believe we can't do anything and begin to feel bad about ourselves. A negative self-concept grows.

The importance of development and self-concept is extremely critical in the growth of children. A self-concept begins very early in life based on how capable we feel we are in pleasing our parents. After all, children want to please the very people they are dependent upon. When the expectations placed on children or infants are inappropriate, that is, they can't complete the task or do the activity because they are too young and don't have the skills, children see themselves as failures. Failures are children who can't seem to please mom and dad no matter how hard they try. When mom and dad are not pleased, they don't offer any praise. Without praise from mom and dad, it is nearly impossible for children to feel good about themselves and develop positive self-concepts. Without positive self-concepts, the chances of children trying new tasks or being successful are slim. This failure carries over to school where children will often see themselves as incapable and less bright than the other children.

What is Important to Learn

Listed in the following pages is information about developmental stages that you should know. Having knowledge of what your children can or can't do will help you in having appropriate developmental expectations of your children. In turn, you will encourage your children to meet success and reinforce positive feelings about themselves.

Developmental Summaries

The following developmental summaries of children serve as a rough guide to normal child development. The lists serve only as a summary and are not a complete index of all the things children can do at any given stage. Children born with birth problems such as prematurity, low birth weight, or illness may not be able to do the things that other children can do who didn't have problems at birth. Most likely, such children will be behind and will need more time to catch up. Only with the support of their family will handicapped children, or children with special developmental needs, grow to the fullest of their capabilities.

Knowing what to expect from your child will lead to success.

Development Stage: Infancy
Chronological Age: Birth to One Year

The first year of an infant's life is both fascinating and startling. For years, psychologists have thought that babies were incompetent creatures who were unable to comprehend the world around them. Today we know that is untrue. At six to ten days, the newborn can recognize the mother by her smell. Some studies reveal that newborns can move their bodies in rhythm to the meaningful speech of adults. Babies at two weeks will look at their own mothers more frequently than they will look at strangers. It is apparent that very young infants can begin to make some sense of their new environment. As they grow older during their first year of life, their body language, intelligence, and social interactions also increase.

Physical Development

The major part of the infant's first year is devoted to survival. The infant is completely helpless at birth and is totally dependent upon the parents for help. Being fed, held, touched, looked at, and talked to have significant impact on the growth of the child. There is so much activity that the average baby sleeps from 16 to 20 hours each day. In fact, there is so much going on during the first year that it is impossible to notice everything. The first year is indeed an important one for the child's physical growth.

- Automatic reflexes such as hand-to-mouth. (0-2 months)
- Will use eyes to follow you. (2 months)
- Will lift head when on his stomach. (2 months)
- Sucks his fingers. (2 months)
- May be pulled slowly by hands to a sitting position. (2 months)
- May be starting to teethe. (4 months)
- Can sit up by himself for short time. (7 months)
- Can begin to crawl by pulling self forward with arms and dragging legs and stomach. (7 months)
- With help of furniture, can pull self up to stand. (7 months)
- Likes to pick things up and drop them only to pick them up again. (7 months)
- Feeds himself pieces of food with hands. (7 months)
- Starts practicing walking but continues crawling. (10 months)
- Likes to eat meals using fingers, using one hand more than the other. (10 months)
- Begins a tottering walk with legs wide apart. (12 months)
- Sits independently on hard surface. (12 months)

Intellectual Development

Closely related are physical and intellectual development. The child learns about the world through exploration of objects, by moving around, and through interactions with the parents. Jean Piaget, a Swiss psychologist, helped us understand how children learn. He believed that intelligence involves adaptation to the world. Such adaptation means that the individual is capable of interacting effectively with the environment. The behavior of infants during the first year, and subsequent years, is to help them understand, adapt, and interact effectively with their world.

- The language of a newborn is crying. Crying occurs without tears for a special reason: to have his/her needs met. (0 - 2 months)

- Reflex behaviors, like sucking, are practiced. (0 - 2 months)

- Begins to recognize familiar voices or faces. (2 months)

- Responds to strangers by crying or staring. (2 months)

- Likes repetition of simple acts like sucking, opening and closing hands, etc., for own sake of activity. (2 - 3 months)

- Baby still cries but also laughs out loud. (4 months)

- Can imitate sounds. Watches your mouth with interest when talking. (7 months)

- Child repeats an act to observe change in the environment. Baby kicks mobile to make it go. However, the child does not organize his actions with a purpose; rather, he discovers the goal accidentally in the process of activity. (6 - 8 months)

- Follows moving objects with eyes. (0 - 12 months)

- Child uses responses to solve problems and to achieve some goal. For example, a child may move one object to get at another. (12 months)

- Responds to and imitates facial expressions of others. (5 - 12 months)

Infants can respond to facial expressions of others.

Language Development

Language develops very slowly during the first year of life. At birth, babies cannot say anything. By the end of their first year, the vocabulary increases to about three words. Even though language is not present during the first year, the experiences the baby has form a crucial basis for the development of language during years one through four.

Babies, however, do communicate their needs even without language. Crying is a way babies let their parents know they are either wet, hungry, tired, or frightened. Mothers and fathers soon learn the difference between a cry of fear and one of hunger. By the second month, babies begin cooing—a way of showing their pleasure. Babbling begins during the fourth or fifth months. Babies repeat syllables over and over again. Parents who talk to, praise, and reinforce their baby's efforts at communication, help the development of language.

- Responds to speech by looking at speaker. (0 - 12 months)

- Makes crying and non-crying sounds. (0 - 12 months)

- Babbles by repeating some vowel and consonant sounds. (0 - 12 months)

- Attempts to imitate sounds. (0 - 12 months)

- Babies begin to "understand" many words or phrases such as "No, come, bring," etc. (12 months)

Infants attempt to imitate sounds and understand some words.

Social/Emotional Development

Erik Erickson describes the stages of social and emotional growth. In the earliest stage, birth to one year, the child struggles with learning to trust or mistrust himself and others in his environment. The degree to which a child comes to trust the environment, other people, and himself depends considerably upon the quality of care the child receives. The child who gets his needs met, his discomforts and fears quickly removed, held, loved, played with, and talked to develops a belief that the world is a safe place. People are dependable and helpful. The child who gets rejected and receives inconsistent and inadequate care develops a basic mistrust of others, his environment, and self. For this child, the world is not a safe, fun place to be. The child feels he cannot depend upon people to have his needs met. Although the child is actively involved in developing trust or mistrust in the first year, the same issue arises again at each successive stage of development.

- Likes high-pitched voices and will usually quiet down when he/she hears them. (0 - 2 months)

- Smiles spontaneously. (0 - 2 months)

- Loves to be played with and likes to be picked up. (4 months)

- Responds differently to strangers (may cry) than to familiar persons. (4 - 6 months)

- Babies may give joyful kicks and gurgle and laugh to engage mother in play. (5 months)

- Knows that mother exists even though she may not be visually present. (5 months)

- May become attached to particular toy. Play time is important. (7 months)

- Child is beginning to learn to be independent. He or she may crawl away from you, but will quickly return. (10 months)

- Child will express anger (through crying) if some wish for mastering a task is frustrated. (8 - 10 months)

- Child loves an audience and will repeat any behavior that gets it. (12 months)

- Tantrums may occur. Based on needs and limited abilities, a child may desire to have or do something that he cannot achieve. (12 months)

Child may have a favorite toy. Playtime is important.

Development Stage: Toddler
Chronological Age: One Year to Three Years

Life with toddlers is rarely dull. Their busyness, intensity, curiosity, independence, and increasing verbal skills make them both exciting and frustrating for parents. Parents are often pleased by some of the observations they verbalize, and sometimes outraged at their stubbornness.

This stage has often been called the "terrible twos" because of the child's increased needs to explore the surroundings and gain control over the environment. Both expressive language and physical mobility increase during this stage. The toddler is in a rush to discover his/her new style of living.

Physical Development

By the end of the first year, the average one year old is between 27 to 29 inches in height and weighs about 22 pounds. By the end of the third year, height has increased to around 36 inches and weight to 35 pounds. Although growth in the second and third years is slower than infancy, it still occurs at a rapid pace.

Large Muscle Development (Gross Motor)

- The child should be walking better. Feet are more parallel and he can walk without holding arms up for balance. Child usually can walk backwards. (15 months)

- The toddler can pick up things from a standing position without falling. Now that hands are free, he loves to carry things, especially big things. (15 - 18 months)

- Child likes to push or pull toys, loves to throw things. (15 - 18 months)

- Seats self in child's chair; moves to music. (18 - 24 months)

- Runs, jumps, climbs, and stands on chair, walks upstairs, crawls downstairs backwards, kicks at ball, loves pounding, tugging, lugging, dumping. (18 - 24 months)

- Climbs small ladder. (around 36 months)

- Walks on tiptoe; stands on one foot with aid. (24 - 36 months)

Child can stand on one foot with aid.

Small Muscle Development (Fine Motor)

- Combines use of several objects: hitting one object with the other; dropping small things into large containers. (15 - 18 months)

- Begins to use spoon to eat; drinks from a cup that is held. (18 months)

- Turns several pages at a time; can make a straight stroke with pencil or crayon instead of just a scribble. (18 months)

- Can turn a doorknob, builds tower of many blocks. (18 months)

- Turns single pages; drinks from a cup without help. (24 - 36 months)

- Removes shoes, pants, socks, sweater, unzips large zipper. (24 months)

- Snips with scissors; holds crayons with thumb and fingers, not fists; paints with wrist action, makes dots, lines, circular strokes. (24 - 36 months)

- Uses one hand consistently in most activities. (24 - 36 months)

One hand is used consistently.

Intellectual Development

The increased exploration and discovery of objects within the environment lead to activities that expand the child's understanding of the world. According to Piaget, at eighteen months, the toddler's interest is beyond his body. Toddlers begin to understand that each object has an independent existence and permanence. Such understanding leads to exploration of these objects and how they work. He learns that a chair remains the same whether seen from above, behind, or underneath.

From eighteen months to two years of age, children are limited to immediate experiencing of objects, people, and whatever or whoever else is present at the moment. Children at this stage spend a lot of time staring at objects, people, or events as a means of exploration of the world. The beginning of language use and memory occurs around two years. By three, children are able to remember events, people, and activities they observed in the environment. Memory expands dramatically. It helps him to learn language. During two and three years of age, language develops rapidly, and imaginative and imitative play increases. Children surprise parents at what they are able to remember and imitate later.

- Toddlers are curious about textures—they like to stroke a cat or dog and rub their cheeks against the fur. (18 months)

- Toddlers are attracted to water and toilets and enjoy playing in the bathroom. (18 - 24 months)

- Imitates actions and words of adults. (18 - 24 months)

- Recognizes difference between you and me. (18 - 24 months)

- Has limited attention span; accomplishes primary learning through exploration of environment. (12 - 24 months)

- Responds to simple directions "give me the block; get your shoes." (24 - 36 months)

- Recognizes self in mirror; can talk briefly about what he is doing. (24 - 36 months)

- Has limited sense of time: vaguely knows idea of past and future and knows such terms as "yesterday" and "tonight," although they may be used incorrectly.

"Hey, that's me!"

Language Development

Babies begin to produce a few basic words at about a year of life. By 24 months, most children are speaking phrases and have a wide range of words. A two-year old has a vocabulary of perhaps 50 words, which increases to about 900 words by the time the child is three.

Many factors contribute to the development of language in a child. A strong, emotional relationship with mother, enhanced by the amount and quality of time spent together, and the amount of talking, asking questions, and responding to what the child says increases the child's verbal activities.

- Says first meaningful words. (12 - 24 months)

- Uses single word plus a gesture to ask for objects. (12 - 24 months)

- Refers to self by name; uses "my" or "mine" to indicate possession. (12 - 24 months)

- Toddler likes to talk to self; replaces baby language with sentences; likes to repeat words. (24 months)

- Joins words together in two word phrases, e.g. "see doggy." (24 months)

- Asks what and where questions. (24 - 36 months)

Social/Emotional Development

Parents of toddlers have an overwhelming job. The child continues to be needy and dependent, but at the same time is growing and developing into an independent person both physically and emotionally. According to Erickson, the second and third years of a child's life focus on the emergence of autonomy. This autonomy is built upon the child's new motor and mental abilities. The child takes pride in his new accomplishments and wants to do everything himself. Whether it is pulling the wrapper off a piece of candy, wanting to dress himself, or flushing the toilet, the child wants to demonstrate his competence at completing the task.

The importance of the stage reflects upon the willingness of parents to allow the child to express his autonomy. If parents are impatient and do for the child what he is capable of doing, they create a sense of shame and doubt. Overprotecting, abusive treatment, criticizing, and inappropriate expectations foster feelings of "I'm not capable" or "I'm not worthy." Such doubt or shame will handicap a child's attempts to achieve autonomy in adolescence and adulthood.

Parents need to help a child explore and grow during this stage. To accomplish this task, parents can:

- Provide a safe environment for the child to explore. "Baby proof" the house. Remove breakables and eliminate hazards.

- Provide a creative environment for the child to explore. Use creative toys and games to facilitate learning.

- Be involved in the child's exploration. Talk to the child to reinforce natural curiosity and exploration of the environment.

Problems

Special social/emotional problems arise during this time that we will briefly discuss.

Separation From Parents

Children quite frequently get upset at separation from their parents, particularly from their mothers. The emotional tie that develops between mother and child results in the child wanting to be with the parent. Crying at separation is normal. Throwing temper tantrums at separation is a sign of possible problems.

Research has shown that children who are positively attached to their mothers develop a sense of trust and feelings of security. Securely attached toddlers are well-liked, outgoing preschoolers who attack new problems vigorously and positively, and can accept help from others. They are sympathetic to others, self-directed and goal-oriented, and exhibit high self-esteem and self-confidence.

Toddlers who are not positively emotionally attached to their parents, particularly to their mothers, exhibit problem behaviors. Such children are anxious, throw more tantrums when presented with problems, and are more negative in response to their mothers. They ignore and oppose their mothers in many ways. Children who feel less securely attached to mom fear separation. The fear can turn into panic during actual separation. To minimize the fear, establish a strong attachment between mother and child. Develop feelings of security and express assurances that mother will not abandon the child.

Establish a strong attachment with your child.

Assertiveness

As the toddler becomes more aware of self, more independent, and more definite in what he can and cannot do, the child will become more assertive in interactions with parents and peers. "No" becomes a common word. "I want," "I need," and "More" are other phrases and words frequently expressed in the toddler years. Children also like to command parents, sometimes adopting dictatorial tones of "Do this" or "Do that!"

Assertion turns to frustration and anger when the toddler cannot accomplish what he or she set out to do. When parents exert limits (discipline) designed to manage the child's behavior, the child may express his anger physically—yelling, crying, temper tantrums, holding breath, or throwing objects. The physical activities release the tension that the child cannot express in words. Consistent application of ignoring undesirable behavior, praising desirable behavior, and punishing unacceptable behavior through time-out, loss of privilege, etc. will help the toddler negotiate this stage of development. As children become more capable and competent at achieving their ends, the tantrums will decrease.

Toilet Training

Most experts agree that somewhere between 18 to 24 months, children are ready to learn how to use a potty chair. However, it is important for parents to know that, just like eating, toileting is an area that parents cannot control. This is the first area children learn that they can control. Therefore, in an extreme struggle of wills in toilet training, the child will win. An approach that helps the child lessen his need to control this area is more successful. Several hints are offered:

1. Three guidelines exist for determining a child's readiness for toilet training:

   - Bladder control—the ability to stay dry for several hours

   - Physical readiness—the ability to get to the toilet and pull pants down

   - Instruction readiness—the ability to understand instructions and communicate needs

2. Don't make a big deal out of toilet training. Do not talk about it much, or give much praise. The child can use the achievement to frustrate parents if he gets angry.

3. Establish a toilet routine. There are many books available on how to establish such a routine.

4. Use a potty chair. It is less frightening than a toilet.

5. Have the child observe the parent or sibling in the bathroom as a model.

Establish a good toilet routine.

Development Stage: Preschool
Chronological Age: Three Years to Six Years

The preschool period in a child's life is an exciting time. During this time, the child reaches out to the world beyond his/her home. For them, the world is an exciting place with many things to do, touch, experience, and eat. Although the preschool child cannot read, write, or compute logical processes, the quest for knowledge overrides any developmental limitations. The preschool years set the stage for experiences, friends, and accomplishments obtained outside the home.

Physical Development

In comparison to earlier stages of development, the physical growth of the preschool child has slowed down considerably. Nevertheless, preschoolers usually gain 2 1/2 to 3 inches in height each year, and three to five pounds in weight. By the age of five years, preschoolers are generally 42" tall and 40 to 45 pounds in weight. The physical growth of the brain achieves about 90% of its adult size around the age of five years.

The growth of the brain helps control voluntary movements. Old skills are refined and elaborated, and are put to new use. The basic motor abilities are present.

Large Muscle Development (Gross Motor)

- Takes longer steps when running or walking. (5 years)

- Catches large ball. (4 - 5 years)

- Skips on one foot. (4 -5 years)

- Hops on one foot. (4 -5 years)

- Many can broad jump 28 to 35 inches. (5 -6 years)

Preschoolers can catch a large ball and hop on one foot.

Small Muscle Development (Fine Motor)

- Children can draw, use scissors, and begin to color. (4 -6 years)

- Can get close to drawing a person. (5 years)

- Can begin to read, write. (5 - 6 years)

- Copies shapes — can draw square and triangle, probably not a diamond. (5 - 6 years)

- Can paint with broad strokes. (5 -6 years)

Intellectual Development

Preschoolers are intellectually curious and actively seek to learn as much about their environment as they possibly can. According to Piaget, the child is in a stage where he/she learns to represent objects, persons, and perceptions with symbols. Thus, the beginnings of functional language. The child is no longer tied to what is physically present.

Questions begin during the preschool years, first about the names of objects and activities, then about the purpose of routines. Increased questions, dreams, nightmares, and fantasy in play are all indications of advances in intellect.

During the preschool period, children believe everything exists for a purpose, even themselves. As such, the child's questions usually reflect such interest: "Mommy, why is there rain? Where do babies come from? Where was I before I was born? Do I have to die?" David Elkind, a noted child psychologist, suggests that parents answer such questions for purpose or function. "It rains to make the trees and flowers grow; babies come from mommies; before you were born, you were just a thought with your mommy and daddy; we all get old and eventually have to die." When the child receives a response that suggests a function or purpose, he is usually satisfied.

"Daddy, why does it rain?"

Preschool children have limited concepts of things and only pay attention to a small number of characteristics. For example, if they see water poured from a short, fat glass to a tall, thin glass the children will say there is more water in the tall one, even though no water was added. Preschoolers cannot easily understand relational terms such as "longer" or "smaller" unless the objects compared are very different.

Language Development

Preschool children are active conversationalists. As they develop intellectually, their language usage increases.

- Vocabulary of about 900 words at three years, 2,000 words at five to six years.

- By the age of five years, children use complete sentences strung together with conjunctions.

- Although they speak clearly, children will have problems with pronunciation and stuttering. These problems are usually temporary and a normal part of development.

- Experiments with sounds, often making up rhyming words. (3 - 6 years)

- Uses "because, how, why" in his efforts to interpret cause and effect. (4 -6 years)

- Conversations tend to be one-sided. (4 - 6 years)

- Children love to giggle with "toilet talk," i.e. words such as "poo poo, pee pee," etc. It's not until years later that children learn to adapt conversation to suit the company.

Social/Emotional Development

Preschoolers are highly social beings. They are ready to reach out and interact with other children in a more responsive fashion. A sense of self as a person; an "I" who thinks, feels, and acts is ready to interact in a more assertive way with his/her environment.

Initiative vs. Guilt

The social dimension that appears during this stage is **initiative**, at one pole, and **guilt** at the other. According to Erickson, children initiate activities due mainly to their gaining mastery of the abilities. This holds true for motor, language, and play activities.

Whether the child will leave this stage with a sense of initiative or sense of guilt depends to a considerable extent on how parents respond to self-initiated activities. Children given freedom to initiate motor, language, and play activities have their sense of initiative reinforced. On the other hand, if the child is made to feel his/her motor activities are bad, questions are a nuisance, and play is silly or stupid, guilt over self-initiated activities will develop that could persist through later life stages.

"I am going to put this puzzle together now."

Play/Imaginary Friends

By age five, children can play cooperatively in a small group. When children aren't available to play with, they invent imaginary companions to fill the void. Imaginary friends are fairly common beginning around age three. Children who have imaginary companions are often bright, creative, verbal, more cooperative, and more aggressive than children who do not. The existence of imaginary friends suggests that children generate the kinds of experiences they need for their own development the environment cannot provide.

Sex Roles and Identity

Most preschoolers play with both boys and girls, but by age six prefer friends of their own sex. Girls imitate their mothers; boys try hard to act like men.

This stage describes the time the Oedipal complex emerges. According to Freud, the child desires to be romantically involved with the parent of the opposite sex—to marry that parent and to have children. Preschool girls can be coy and charming to dad. Preschool boys can be protective and seductive with mom. During this period, preschoolers often feel competitive with the same sex parent, sometimes wishing the parent dead. Parents should remain supportive and understanding of the child. Eventually, the sexual identities change where sons and daughters often wish to be just like dad and mom.

Nighttime Wetting

Children usually have learned to be potty trained around three years of age. However, accidents can happen and do, usually at night.

Nighttime wetting is more common among boys than girls, largely due to the nervous system of boys maturing more slowly. Ask the child how he thinks the problem could be solved. Some possible solutions are not drinking liquids after dinner, going to the bathroom just before bedtime, or not changing the sheets until morning. Again, the parents should remain supportive and give the child encouragement. Scolding or punishment will not solve the problem.

Excessive Masturbation

Although masturbation is a normal behavior, excessive masturbation can be a concern. Excessive masturbation may be the result of an unhappy, anxious child. Finding the sources of the unhappiness and anxiety, and correcting them, is a first step.

Often excessive masturbation in children results from not being a part of a social group. Providing many opportunities for activities with peers, helping the child achieve feelings of competence, and parental support often ends the problem.

Fears

Fears are a natural part of growing up. During the preschool years, children often fear animals, the dark, imaginary creatures, and natural events like storms, fires, thunder, and lightning. Parents who criticize a child for his fears, who are sarcastic, or even punish a child for having fears are not helping to reduce the fears. These tactics decrease the self-confidence and self-esteem of the child. A model of confident, nonfearful behavior, discussion of the fear, support, and understanding from the parents help the child to understand the fear. This will eventually diminish the fear to a more manageable level.

Baby Proofing Your House

Children, especially young toddlers, love to explore. Touching, pulling, grabbing, and eating are just a few of the ways young children explore their environment. Since toddlers are too young to know what is safe to play with and what is potentially dangerous, parents baby proof their house. Baby proofing protects children from becoming hurt, or in some instances, even killed.

Parents also baby proof their house to enhance the positive interactions they have with their children. A house where dangerous objects are out of reach is a house where parents aren't constantly saying no.

Is Your House Baby Proofed?

You probably wonder at times whether your house is safe enough for your toddler to play in without a high risk for injury. There are two things you can do to see if your house is safe for toddlers:

1. Get down on your hands and knees and view the world as a toddler. What you can pull, grab, bite, so can your child. Move tempting and dangerous objects out of reach.

View your house as a toddler. Watch your child explore.

2. Watch your child as he explores his environment. Walk with your child through the house and notice what he notices. Can he reach that shelf? Can he push that button? Can he climb that chair? You'll soon find out by watching him. If he can reach objects he shouldn't, it's time to better baby proof your house.

Once Baby Proofed, Always Baby Proofed?

You only need to baby proof your house once, right? Wrong! Babies grow along with their ability to reach for objects, climb on furniture, open drawers, and walk up and down stairs. You will continually need to modify your house as your child continues to grow. The good news is that as your child grows older, he's also learning what is safe and what isn't.

Safety Checklist

The following safety checklist is designed to ensure your house is safe enough for your toddler to play in with only minimal risk of injury. Take some time now to go over this checklist, room by room, to make your house safe for your child. Make it a habit to recheck your house at least once a month.

All Rooms

To Do	Action	Done
( )	1. Put electric outlet covers on all unused outlets.	( )
( )	2. Put a gate across all stairways, top and bottom, until child can handle stairs.	( )
( )	3. Remove or pad sharp corners on furniture and appliances.	( )
( )	4. Remove throw rugs on tiled floors.	( )
( )	5. Use non-skid floor wax on wood, tile, or linoleum floors.	( )
( )	6. Keep all plants out of baby's reach.	( )

Kitchen

To Do	Action	Done
( )	1. Put all cleaning supplies on a top shelf out of children's reach.	( )
( )	2. Install safety locks on all kitchen cabinets below waist level. You may want to keep one cabinet with pots, pans, and unbreakable bowls unlocked for child's exploration.	( )
( )	3. Turn pot handles toward back of stove when cooking.	( )
( )	4. Take knobs off of gas ranges when not in use.	( )
( )	5. Have a secure cover for the garbage can.	( )
( )	6. Install safety locks on kitchen drawers with knives and other sharp utensils.	( )
( )	7. Keep all breakable bowls out of the cabinets with the pots and pans.	( )
( )	8. Remove throw rugs from kitchen floors.	( )
( )	9. Make sure highchairs are stable and have safety straps.	( )
( )	10. Remove tablecloth to prevent toddlers from pulling it off.	( )
( )	11. Keep items in use such as glasses, jars, bowls, utensils, etc. well back on the kitchen counter.	( )
( )	12. Remove pet food bowls to an area inaccessible to your baby.	( )

Bathroom

To Do	Action	Done
( )	1. Store all electrical appliances such as hair dryers, curling irons, electric toothbrushes in the bathroom cabinet or closet.	( )
( )	2. Put safety locks on all bathroom cabinets.	( )
( )	3. Remove all electrical appliances near water.	( )
( )	4. Place a non-skid bath mat on the bottom of tub.	( )
( )	5. Buy a rubber safety cover for the bathtub water faucets and spout to prevent accidental head injuries and scalding.	( )
( )	6. Keep all medicine in a locked medicine cabinet.	( )

Living Room

To Do	Action	Done
( )	1. Secure lamps and other freestanding objects.	( )
( )	2. Fence off fireplaces, wood stoves, space heaters, radiators, and heating grates.	( )
( )	3. Remove all breakable knickknacks and ashtrays.	( )
( )	4. Lock all gun cabinets.	( )
( )	5. Attach electrical lamp cords and extension cords to tables or baseboards.	( )
( )	6. Remove coffee table and other sharp-edged furniture from child's access and play areas.	( )

Bedrooms

To Do	Action	Done
( )	1. Install a night light for nighttime trips to the bathroom.	( )
( )	2. Move furniture and cribs away from windows.	( )
( )	3. Place safety locks on all windows and screens.	( )
( )	4. Make sure bars on cribs are no more than 2 1/2 inches apart.	( )
( )	5. Make sure mattress fits bed frame snugly.	( )
( )	6. Install bumper pads on inside of crib for young infants, the soft kind that bends or folds when stood on.	( )
( )	7. Remove mobiles over bed once child is capable of sitting or pulling to sit.	( )

Basement, Garage, Attic

To Do	Action	Done
( )	1. Throw away all old paints you're not using. Store paint thinners, paint, stains, etc. on a high shelf if you need to keep them.	( )
( )	2. Store all tools in a locked tool chest or shelved out of reach.	( )
( )	3. Lock all doors securely.	( )
( )	4. Keep garden tools, lawn mowers, snow blowers out of reach of young children.	( )
( )	5. Keep keys to electric machines safely out of reach.	( )
( )	6. Take doors off of old refrigerators and freezers.	( )
( )	7. Store pesticides and fertilizers on high shelves out of reach of children.	( )

General Safety Rules

1. Never leave a young child unattended in the bathroom.

2. Install smoke alarms and fire extinguishers.

3. Keep all matches and candles out of reach.

4. Post emergency numbers beside the telephone.

5. Never refer to medication as candy.

6. Avoid letting children play with small objects he/she can swallow.

7. Never leave a young child unattended in the basement, garage, or attic.

8. Keep ashtrays and cigarette butts out of children's reach. Nicotine is a deadly poison when eaten.

Safety Reminders By Age

1 month – Crib Check

Make sure there is no space between mattress and crib side for baby to get caught. Use bumper pads.

2 months – Guard Against Falls

Babies can roll over already. Never leave a child unattended on a dressing table or other high place.

3 months – Car Seats

Always use a properly installed car seat. If you also use the seat outside of the car, prevent falls by never putting it above floor level.

4 months – Guard Against Choking

Do not give young children small objects or pieces of hard food such as peanuts, popcorn, or hard candy. Learn the approved anti-choking maneuver for children from your pediatrician.

5 months – Guard Against Scalds

Babies like to grab and hit at things in your hands. Do not drink or carry hot liquids when near or holding a baby.

6 months – Sitting Alone

Baby may sit alone – but not in the bathtub. Never leave a child unattended in or near water.

7 months – Safe Exploring

Keep dangerous or breakable objects up and out of young crawler's exploring reach.

8 months – Pulling Up

Watch for falls. Check crib for areas where baby may catch his head or neck.

9 months – Avoid Shocks

Block electrical plugs with approved safety devices.

10 months – Bigger Car Seat

Switch to toddler car seat and use it every time child is in car.

11 months – Burns

In the kitchen, hot liquids, grease, and hot foods are a danger. So are irons, hot stoves, radiators, heating registers, and fireplaces.

12 months – Stairway Safety

Watch open doors and stairs. Use gates at top and bottom of steps.

13 months — Walking and Exploring

Beware of poisoning danger from houseplants, household chemicals, and medicines. Keep syrup of Ipecac, poison control phone number, and first aid chart and supplies handy.

14 months — Climbing

Children can now climb on chairs and tables — and find more danger. Keep medications and cleaning fluids out of reach. Use safety tops on all bottles and jars. Put locks on cabinets and drawers.

16 months — Exploring Outdoors

Define play areas and make them safe and interesting. Guard against scratches and bites from stray cats and dogs.

18 months — Water Play

Avoid hot water burns — keep water temperature between 120 degrees and 130 degrees F. Never leave a child alone in a tub or near any quantity of water — even a pail or a puddle — even if the child has had "swimming" lessons.

2 years — Expanding Limits

Start teaching good pedestrian habits and the limits of the child's "territory."

3 years — Riding a Tricycle

Driveways and streets are dangerous. Allow riding only in fenced yards or playgrounds.

4 years — Venturing Further

Teach good pedestrian habits — look both ways, stay out from between parked cars.

5 years — Bigger and Bigger

You can now switch to seat belts for your child. Don't forget to "buckle up" yourself every time, too.

6 years — Riding a Bicycle

Watch for falls. Teach good bicycle and street safety.

Information from the American Academy of Pediatrics Committee on Accident and Poison Prevention, Growing Parent & Growing Child, October 1984, Vol. 12 No. 10, Dunn & Hargitt, Inc.

Recognizing and Understanding Feelings

Feelings have been written about, sung about, and discussed more than any other aspect of our lives. It is not surprising many people feel that recognizing our own feelings and the feelings of our children is the single most important part of being a nurturing parent.

There are two categories feelings fall into: comfort and discomfort. Positive feelings of comfort like joy, love, peace, security, and happiness give us courage by reaffirming what is right—what is good. Good comes from good, and feelings of comfort encourage us and our children to give our best. They build a sense of self-worth. Knowing what makes us feel happy can often help us to quit sitting around and feeling sorry for ourselves.

Positive feelings build a sense of self-worth.

Feelings of discomfort like anger, hatred, envy and jealousy limit our ability to see the world as a positive place to live. Instead, feelings of discomfort paint the world a dull gray, with unhappiness. Feelings of discomfort limit rather than build positive self-esteem in us and our children. If at times during the program you feel a resistance against answering questions regarding your past hurts, please know this is natural. You may also feel resistance against letting others know your painful feelings, this is also very natural. People wish to avoid pain. Talking about past hurts usually brings up past pain; but not talking about the past and hurts never helps. It only causes more problems. Let's see why.

Learning and Feeling

Every experience we have leaves us with both thoughts and feelings. It really makes no difference what the experience is, we will think and feel something about it when the experience is over.

For example, let's take an experience like going out on a blind date. Whether our blind date looks and acts like the handsome prince or gorgeous princess, or looks and acts like the frog, we will definitely remember the experience as being either good or terrible. If the blind date was a lot of fun and we had a good time, we will probably go out with that person again. What we learned was that taking a risk and going out with a stranger was okay because we had a good time. If the time together with the blind date turned out to be a real drag, we would probably choose not to go out with that person again. We probably would not even risk going out on another blind date again simply because we learned that taking risks by going out with a stranger was not okay. In either case, we learned and felt something from the experience.

Painful Past Experiences

When experiences in our lives have been very painful, many of us do not want to deal with the pain. We avoid dealing with the pain either consciously or unconsciously. Since we don't want to or are unable to handle the pain, somehow we have to get rid of it. Some examples of painful experiences could be the death of a loved one, the breakup of a meaningful relationship, or some painful experience in childhood. In these instances, and many others like them, we will try to forget the experience altogether. We may also attempt to get rid of the painful feelings. Neither works very well in the long run. The painful feelings don't go away, they're just out of sight — but there nonetheless.

As children we learn not to feel pain, not to cry, not to recognize our discomforts. We learn that boys don't cry, and little girls have to be little ladies who are pretty, neat, and clean. We learn very early in life not to deal with pain or other feelings of discomfort.

What Happens to Painful Feelings

Think of experiences that you had in your childhood, or are having now, that have been or are very painful. Now, think of the experience as a big spring, the kind you find in box springs, and in cushioned chairs and couches. The natural position of a spring is fully extended. To squash the spring, we have to apply a lot of pressure to keep the spring from being fully extended. Think of each painful experience we have that we are unwilling or unable to handle as a giant spring that we have to squash by stepping on it. And since we don't want to feel the pain of the experience, we constantly have to step on the spring. The moment we let up from stepping on the spring, it becomes fully extended. When we can't control the painful feelings, they come leaping into our conscious mind. When that happens, we re-live the experience again. The goal for many is to keep stepping on the spring and hiding the painful feelings. Just like money you put in your bank account draws interest and grows, so do the painful feelings. They get bigger and bigger until they are taking up a lot of our energy. Since life has many painful experiences that happen naturally, a lot of people spend the majority of their energy stepping on springs trying to hide all painful feelings from experiences. If we spend our energy stepping on springs, we have little left to be nurturing to ourselves and our children. It's as simple as that. To be more nurturing to yourself and others, you have to let the springs up. It means taking a risk by sharing with others past hurts and pain, as well as past joys and pleasures.

Take a risk. Let your springs up and share yourself.

How to Handle Feelings

Feelings are a natural expression of human life. Babies have feelings—so do children, teenagers, and adults. Handling the feelings of comfort like love, joy, and security is no problem for the majority of us. We like those feelings. It's the feelings of discomfort that cause us problems. We don't like to feel pain, hurt, envy, and anger. We hide those feelings, just like the spring.

The absolute best way to handle all feelings is to express them. Feelings want to be expressed. When we feel anger toward another, it is also good to let that person know how angry you are. The main goal of sharing your feelings is always to communicate—not to hurt or cause further pain for you or the other person. In the Nurturing Program, you will learn appropriate ways of expressing your feelings of comfort and discomfort.

"I love you!"

The Four Primary Feelings

We have many words to describe our feelings: joy, embarrassment, rage, depression, excitement, helplessness, anxiety, comfort, etc.

Just as all colors (green, beige, purple, turquoise, etc.) are mixtures of only three basic or "primary colors," our complex feelings are mixtures of only four basic or "primary feelings." The four primary feelings are: **glad, mad, sad, and scared.**

It is helpful to reduce our complex feelings to their primary components. This way we can see more clearly just how to go about meeting our needs. We can understand just what we must do if we wish to change a mad, sad, or scared feeling into a glad feeling.

Physical pain or discomfort lets us know that we must take care of our bodily needs to avoid damage to our bodies. For example, when you feel a burning sensation, you know to take your hand off the stove—quickly! When your body is fighting a germ, you feel feverish and weak. These feelings let you know you must rest and drink fluids.

In the same way, emotional pain or discomfort lets us know that we must take care of our psychological needs, to avoid damage to our spirits. Emotional needs that are not taken care of right away leave psychological scars just as surely as unattended physical needs leave scars on the body.

All human beings have the basic needs to:

- be noticed, recognized, important to others

- belong, have emotional ties

- be safe from harm

The three "uncomfortable" primary feelings (mad, sad, scared) signal us that one of our basic human needs is not being met.

Glad

Glad is the feeling of relief, satisfaction, or freedom from pain. Glad is the one primary feeling which does not represent an unmet need. It is the feeling we have when our needs are satisfied. To keep feeling glad, you must find effective ways to meet your needs.

Example: George realizes that he needs quiet in order to concentrate. He takes care of that need by keeping his office door closed when he has work that requires concentration. He is generally glad to be at work because he is good at taking care of his own needs there.

Find effective ways to meet your needs.

Mad

Mad is the feeling from unfairness or lack of recognition of the importance of needs. Mad is the feeling that we have when the importance of our needs (physical or psychological) is being ignored by others or ourselves. It is a feeling of injustice that our needs do not count, are not important enough to notice. To stop feeling mad, you must correct the injustice by paying close attention to your own needs, taking them into account and asking directly for what you really need and want. This may involve negotiation with others.

Example: Mary, a working wife and mother of small children, was irritable much of the time. She realized she was mad that she never had time to herself anymore, that she was putting the needs of husband and kids first and not taking care of herself. Mary discussed her need with her husband and got him to acknowledge its importance. Through negotiation with him, Mary arranged one evening a week out pursuing her own interests and a couple of hours each weekend in which her husband would take the kids out so she would have the house to herself.

"Tonight is my night. I feel so good!"

Sad

Sad is the feeling from the loss of an important attachment (to a person, place, or thing). Sad is experiencing loss. Attachments are a vital part of human life, and the loss of some of them from time to time is inevitable. To stop feeling sad, you must first allow yourself to experience the loss, acknowledge the importance of the attachment in your life, and then move on. Moving on generally means replacing the lost person, place, or thing by others that can, in whole or in part, meet needs of yours that were once met by the lost one.

Example: Joey's family moved across the country. He was very sad at school and at home because he missed his best friend Jon with whom he used to study and rollerskate. When he moped about, his family recognized how sad he was and tried to be supportive while he worked through his grief. They listened sympathetically when he complained that the kids at school were "dorks." They understood that Joey felt just then that no one could replace Jon. They encouraged him to call and write Jon periodically and arranged for a summer visit. At the same time, they encouraged him to go to the roller rink and did all that they could to make it easy for him to get together with new friends from school. By the end of the school year, Joey became friends with Brian. Both Joey and Brian enjoyed rollerskating and were spending a lot of time at the roller rink.

Scared

Scared is the feeling from lack of safety, threat to future well-being, or inability to structure or control the future. When we feel scared, it is because we believe that we will soon suffer some damage to our bodies or our spirits. To stop feeling scared, you must realistically assess the true potential for damage and set up effective ways to structure your future. We often scare ourselves by assessing the potential damage as much greater than it is. When it is cut down to its proper size, the danger can usually be controlled or eliminated by taking a few simple steps.

Example: Linda hated parties and social gatherings of all kinds. Each time she faced an office party or even a neighborhood get-together, her stomach got upset. If she attended, she would find herself in a corner, unable to speak to anyone, and lonely. When she thought deeply about the matter, she realized that her fantasy about these events was that everyone else was perfectly comfortable and always had interesting things to say. She was afraid that she would bore people and therefore would not be liked and would end up lonely. To assess the real danger, she checked with a few close friends and found out the following: they thought she had interesting things to say and was not a boring person; they, and many others they knew, were sometimes uncomfortable in groups; people like as much (or more) to be listened to as talked to; and, her friends valued her listening skills. Linda decided that the next time she had to attend a gathering, she would adopt the following strategy: read the newspapers to inform herself about current news and cultural events; begin to interact with others by listening closely and asking questions of them; and, not expect herself to interact with everyone in the room, but to mainly focus on the few people who most attracted her. Over time, Linda found that she had become quite adept and comfortable at parties and no longer felt scared of loneliness.

Control your scared feelings.

Praising Yourself and Your Children

Praise is a word, gesture, expression on your face, or statement that promotes pride, joy, and accomplishment in children. Praise is a way of giving children feelings of positive feedback to increase their sense of worth, competence, and confidence.

In praising children, you are pointing out the worth of their abilities, traits, or achievements. When your child tries hard at doing something, even if he doesn't finish, praise the effort. When your daughter brings home a completed project, praise the work. When your child looks good, tell him or her. When children do things that are pleasing, let them know. Praise your children daily.

Praise for Being and Praise for Doing

There are two primary areas to use praise. One area we call praise for being and the other area we call praise for doing.

Praise for being is the highest form of praise. It tells children that just because they are your son or daughter they have value and are worth praise. Praise for being lets children know you value them for just who they are.

Some praise for being statements are:

- "I really love you!"
- "What a pretty smile."
- "What a special child you are."
- "I am so happy you are my son."
- "You're a wonderful daughter."

When you praise others for being, they don't have to do anything to earn it.

Praise for doing lets children know you appreciate and highly value their efforts and behaviors. Praise for doing praises a child's behavior; praise for being praises a child. Children love to please their parents. When they hear praise for doing something, they know they pleased mom and dad. Praising a child's behavior can be for something they tried and completed, or tried but didn't quite succeed or finish. Acknowledge children's efforts and they are more apt to try again.

Some praise for doing statements are:

- "What a good job cleaning your room."
- "I'm really pleased to see you try so hard."
- "You buttoned all you buttons. Good for you."
- "I'm so proud of the way you cooperated."
- "You made pee pee all by yourself. What a big boy!"

Using Praise Incorrectly

Many parents unknowingly use praise incorrectly by using praise for being and praise for doing together. Such statements as:

- "What a nice job cleaning your room. Mommy really loves you."

or

- "Daddy really loves you for cooperating with me."

Such statements only tell children you love or appreciate them only when they do something that pleases mom or dad. It's known as "conditional love" — love that has to be earned. Children quickly learn to resent such love because they know if they don't "do something," mommy or daddy won't love them.

Some parents use praise as a weapon or something they can take away at a moment's notice. Such statements like:

- "If you don't cooperate, I'm not gonna love you anymore."

or

- "If you want me to be nice to you, you better eat all your food."

How horrible these statements are! Young children are so dependent on their parents' love for feelings of security and dependency! Threats to take their love away only ends up teaching children that it is not good to love someone, or please someone because "When I mess up, mommy or daddy threaten to take their love away." Many children have difficulty getting close to another person. They feel they have to "pay for" the love of another. Avoid using praise incorrectly and inappropriately.

Praising Your Self

Many people feel awkward at the thought of praising themselves. Often, there is confusion between self-praise and being conceited. The two are completely different. Self-praise is your own personal way of recognizing yourself for being and for doing. Essentially, you are telling yourself that as a person you always have value. Even though you may mess up by failing a test or by hurting someone else, you have value. Being conceited means that you believe you are better than someone else. Being better makes others "less than." People don't like being told they are "less than you" and will resent you for it. Self-praise means your value as a person is always high — but not in comparison to others.

"I did a nice job making supper tonight."

Promoting Self-Praise in Children

Self-praise is a way children can learn the habit of praising themselves and boosting up their self-image. To help a child learn self-praise, parents need to describe how good the act must have made the child feel. Imagine yourself in the child's shoes, and describe the feeling. By promoting self-praise, children develop an internal evaluation process that is both realistic and genuine.

"Tracie, you must feel good after cleaning your room."

To encourage children to use self-praise, parents should model the behavior for them. Praise yourself in the presence of your children whenever you do something well, or whenever you feel proud of some effort. Modeling self-praise is an effective teaching procedure because children learn best by imitation.

How to Praise

To praise appropriately, follow the steps listed below:

1. **Focus your attention on the child and the situation—praise deserves your undivided attention.**

2. **Move close to the child—praise feels good by someone close to you.**

3. **Make eye contact with the child on the child's level. For instance, stoop down to make eye-contact with a two-year old—this makes it all the more special.**

4. **Gently touch the child—touch is a positive form of communication.**

5. **Look pleasant—everyone likes to see a happy face.**

6. **Praise your child for being or for doing.**

7. **Offer a hug to "seal" the nice words.**

Praise anytime—there is no such thing as too much praise.

Our Self-Esteem and Self-Concept

Everyone has a self-esteem. A self-esteem is how we feel about ourselves. Recognizing how we feel about ourselves is important because we base our beliefs on the way we feel. When we feel good about ourselves (high self-esteem), we are more capable of treating others the same way—good. When we feel bad about ourselves (low self-esteem), we are also more capable of treating others the same way—badly.

Working on keeping our self-esteem high will help us be nice and nurturing to others: our children, friends, spouses, and co-workers.

Everyone also has a self-concept. A self-concept is what we think about ourselves. Being aware of what we think of ourselves is also important because, along with our feelings, our thoughts guide our behavior. We use our knowledge of ourselves to make choices, decisions, problem solve, and identify right from wrong. If we don't think highly of ourselves (low self-concept) the choices and decisions we make will reflect our low self-concept. When we feel like a loser we will act like a loser, and others will treat us accordingly—like a loser.

When we think highly of ourselves (high self-concept), the choices and decisions we make will tell everyone we think we're winners. A winner is someone who thinks good things about him/herself and acts that way. When you think of yourself as a winner, people treat you that way, and you in turn treat others as winners.

A positive self-concept and a healthy self-esteem together are primarily responsible for the way we believe.

Babies begin to develop a self-concept and a self-esteem right from birth. As parents, our goal is to provide the best possible environment for children to grow up thinking and feeling positively toward themselves. The techniques that you are learning in the Nurturing Program will help you be the best parent you can be. We're glad you're in the Nurturing Program.

Words I use to describe my self-concept are:

1. _____
2. _____
3. _____
4. _____
5. _____

Words I use to describe my self-esteem are:

1. _____
2. _____
3. _____
4. _____
5. _____

Needs of Adults, Adolescents, and Children

Whether we are adults, adolescents, or children, we all have the same area of needs.

Physical Needs

The need for sleep, food, exercise, air, water, and sex.

Emotional Needs

The need for love, praise, feeling worthwhile, security, trust, and self-regard.

Social Needs

The need for friendship and companionship. Usually sought from our peer group.

Intellectual Needs

The need for intellectual stimulation, thinking new thoughts, reading challenging books, and learning something new.

Spiritual Needs

The need to know that we are part of something bigger than ourselves and that we can increase our awareness and the sensitivity to the greater aspects of life.

Creative Needs

The need to express self: to make something, dance, or write a poem.

Areas of needs.

I Statements and You Messages

I statements are expressions about me. These expressions can focus on how I feel, what I need, or about what I think. For example, I statements about how I feel may be: I feel angry; I feel excited; or, I feel depressed. I statements about what I need may be: I need a hug; I need a glass of water; or, I need some quiet time. I statements about what I think could be: I think I will not go; I think I am lost; or I think the team should trade for a good quarterback. I statements make me the center of attention — the star of the moment. I statements focus on me, tell about me, and describe me.

I statements make you the center of attention — the star.

You messages are about someone else. They are your perceptions of how someone else feels, about what someone else needs, or about what someone else thinks. Some examples of you messages regarding someone else's feelings could be: You look angry; you seem excited; or, you appear depressed. You messages regarding someones needs could be: You need a hug; you need a glass of water; or, you need some quiet time. You messages regarding someone's thoughts could be: What do you think about nuclear energy? Do you think the team should trade for a good quarterback? You messages make someone else the center of attention — the star of the moment. You messages focus on someone else, tell about someone else, or describe someone else. The big difference is that messages about someone else are only guesses or perceptions about how they look, how they feel, or what they need. Only that person knows for sure if the you messages are accurate.

Ownership of Feelings

The main difference between I statements and you messages centers on ownership. When used appropriately, I statements convey ownership of feelings, thoughts, and needs. Each person is responsible for his or herself.

That is, no one can make you feel, think, or need something you don't want. Although others can influence your decision, the final say belongs to you and no one else.

When people use I statements, they are essentially taking ownership of what they feel, think, or need. Taking ownership of your own feelings, thoughts, and needs is the first step in using I statements appropriately.

You messages cannot express ownership of feelings simply because no one can own anyone else's feelings, thoughts, and needs. Ownership is a highly individualistic concept.

Appropriate and Inappropriate Use of I Statements

Use of I statements is appropriate when a person wants to send some message about him or herself. Such statements convey ownership and represent a clear statement of the person's feelings, thoughts, and needs.

- "I am angry with you because you started a fight with Billie."

- "I am not aware of any restaurant open this time of night."

- "I need to spend some time by myself in order to unwind."

"*I feel excited to be able to go to the beach.*"

I statements are often used inappropriately. Sometimes people make I statements in order to manipulate others into doing something. Some examples of the inappropriate use of I statements may be:

- "I am so upset at what you are doing that I might have a heart attack."

- "If you don't do it my way, I will get a migraine headache."

These statements are manipulative. Their intent is to control someone's behavior. The clear message and the ownership of the feeling is not present.

Appropriate Use of You Messages

You messages are used appropriately in three ways.

To Give Choices

You messages work well in combination with choices and consequences: a message is being sent to the child. The message describes alternative plans of behavior and their expected consequences.

An example may be: "Stephen, you have a choice. You can clean your room now, or you can clean your room later. However, if your room is not cleaned by 6 p.m., you can't watch T.V. tonight. It's your choice."

In this instance, you sent a you message to Stephen, and Stephen was the center of attention. As you already know, giving children choices helps them develop a sense of responsibility.

To Give Praise

You messages work well when praising someone for being or for doing. When praising, the center of attention naturally belongs to someone else. That's the time for a whole string of you messages.

- "You must feel very proud."

- "You must feel really good."

- "You have done that so well."

Letting someone know how proud you are would be good also, as long as the center of attention remains with the other person.

To Gain Clarification

You messages are ideal to send when you desire clarification. As mentioned earlier, you messages are your perceptions or guesses about how another person feels, what another person is thinking, or what another person needs. When a you message requests clarification, we are essentially asking for validation. Are my perceptions right or wrong?

Some examples are:

- "You seem to be really angry."

- "You appear sad."

- "You don't seem to like the play."

The receiver is able to respond to the question(s) based on a quick inventory of how he is feeling. Sending a you message for clarification helps the sender know the state of being of the receiver. It also lets the receiver know how he appears to be acting.

Send you messages to give choices, give praise, or gain clarification.

Inappropriate Use of You Messages

No one likes to have negative or bad feelings. It doesn't feel good to be angry, sad, afraid, depressed, or out of control. All people have these feelings at some time or another during their lives. When we do have negative feelings, it's often difficult to take full responsibility for the feelings. It's easier and much safer to blame someone else for the way we feel. In that way, we don't have to take responsibility for our actions.

Statements like: "You made me angry," "You give me a headache," or "You made me lose control" are good examples of you messages that are blaming. They are the adult version of the child's "He made me do it."

Increasing Family Communication

The appropriate use of I statements and you messages is important for establishing and enhancing communication among family members. The ability to accept and receive praise, to carry out nonabusive behavior management strategies, to listen to the needs, feelings, and thoughts of your children, and to communicate your own feelings, thoughts, and needs all center around your success at using I statements and you messages. The time and energy you invest in learning how to send I statements and you messages will pay rich dividends. They will increase honest communication between you, your children, mate, and friends.

Use I statements and you messages to communicate.

Confrontation and Criticism:
Sweet and Sour Music to My Ears

Communicating our thoughts and feelings is not an easy thing to do. It becomes even more difficult when the information we need to share with someone can hurt their feelings. So, what's a person to do? Well, we have two choices. Our first choice is to say what we have to say to the other person without having any concern about the person's feelings. The first choice is commonly called criticism. In fact, when we criticize, we are often intent on hurting the other person's feelings purposefully. Criticism is a verbally abusive behavior.

The second choice we have in communicating our feelings is called confrontation. To confront someone is to share your feelings and thoughts in a manner that is not intended to cause hurt to someone else. Confrontation is a nurturing behavior. Let's examine the two a little further and find out more about criticism and confrontation.

Criticism

When we criticize others, we are really telling them what they did or didn't do was wrong. It also tells them they are inadequate and bad. There are many things wrong about using criticism. Here are a few:

- **Criticism hurts.** It's supposed to hurt. It's like slapping someone in the face with mean words. It's verbal abuse.

- **Criticism destroys.** Criticism never feels good to the person being criticized because criticism tears people down. Think of criticism as a big crane with a big heavy ball at the end used by construction workers to knock down buildings. After the building is knocked down, all that's left is rubble. Just like the crane and ball, when you constantly criticize someone, all that's left is emotional rubble where once stood a healthy human being.

- **Criticism blames.** No one likes being blamed for something they did or didn't do, regardless of the person's age. Blaming never tells people the right thing to do. It only focuses on the bad — always!

- **Criticism closes people up.** People become defensive. Some act like a mummy. They do nothing, say nothing, and eventually hear nothing. At least not what you're saying. Children especially tune the parents out when they're being critical. Who could blame them for tuning out criticism?

- **Criticism creates anger in others.** Some people respond to criticism by getting angry and start to fight back. Criticism is a common ground of all arguments.

You get the idea I'm sure. When you criticize, you take away. In the end, both you and the person you criticize lose.

Why Do Parents Criticize?

Generally people criticize others out of feelings of inadequacy. When you need to knock someone down verbally, most often they are standing emotionally taller than you. It's often said that what we dislike in others is what we dislike most about ourselves.

Confrontation

To confront others is to let them know your thoughts and feelings in a way that communicates respect for them as human beings. It doesn't tear down, confrontation builds self-respect and gives people information. Here are some reasons why confrontation works better than criticism:

- **Confrontation communicates respect for the other person.** When you confront someone on some issue, you are actually comparing your views with someone else's view.

- **Confrontation helps people listen.** When you have an awkward or painful message to share, confrontation keeps people listening. Criticism shuts people down. You have a better chance of others hearing your message when you use confrontation.

- **Confrontation provides useful information.** People can do something with the information they receive from confrontation. Criticism usually tells people what they haven't done.

- **Confrontation generally promotes a friendship.** True friends confront each other on some issue. They are sensitive to the feelings of others.

- **Confrontation promotes changes.** People don't have to waste valuable energy being defensive and angry. They can get busy doing something about what they're being confronted on.

"What are your views?"

Why Do People Confront?

Confrontation is always based out of respect. People who use confrontation rather than criticism are generally more caring, nurturing, happier people.

Examples of Criticism and Confrontation

You can praise someone for who they are (being) and their behavior (doing). You can also criticize and confront others for being and doing. Let's take some examples:

Criticism:

"You're just a lazy slob. Look at this messy room. What are you, some kind of pig?"

Confrontation:

"Your room needs to be cleaned."

Criticism:

"What the hell did you do that for? You're gonna regret the day you were born!"

Confrontation:

"It looks to me like you made a bad choice of behavior. You know the consequence for your choice!"

Criticism:

"Your breath stinks to high hell. What did you eat—a dead skunk?"

Confrontation:

"I want you to know your breath needs some mouthwash."

Criticism:

"Look at you! You look like a tramp with all that make-up on and crazy hairdo. You're a weirdo!"

Confrontation:

"I think the amount of make-up you have on does not show your real beauty. Maybe you can...."

Criticism:

"Don't stay out late; don't let the guy try anything funny; and don't drink and drive."

Confrontation:

"I expect you home at curfew. I trust that you will be careful and safe. Have a good time."

Constructive Criticism

The term is a fluke. There is no positive value in tearing another person down! When we feel another person would profit from being criticized, all we need to do is to get in touch with the last time someone we cared about criticized us for our own good. We experienced a feeling of hurt, or shame, or anger, or embarrassment, or some other negative feeling. Nurturing people choose to treat others with respect and generate positive feelings.

It's Our Choice

As parents and as teenagers, we have a choice. We can confront others or criticize them. Both are forms of communication although confronting others is more difficult than criticizing. It's easier not to care, to pretend to be better than others, and to project our own inadequacies on others. For many of us, it's far too easy. Let's use our personal power in constructive, growth building ways.

"I think your breath needs some mouthwash."

The Formula for Communicating with I Statements

When you _____
                                (describe the exact behavior)

I feel _____
                                (state a feeling: glad/mad/sad/scared)

because _____
                    (state the need that relates to that feeling and any thought or belief related to it)

What I want is _____
                                (describe the exact behavior that would meet the need)

Examples:

1. When you pick up your things each day, I feel glad because I need to have things tidy in order to feel good about our house. I want to thank you for being so considerate of my need for order, even though it is not your need.

2. When you did not call me yesterday to let me know that you would be home late, I felt scared because I need to know that you are safe. I believe that it is unsafe to walk in that area after dark. What I want is to understand your plan for keeping yourself safe, and to be contacted whenever you are going to get home more than a half hour late.

   I also felt mad because when you did not call, I believed that you did not really care about my need to know you were OK. What I want is to hear from you, know that you understand my need, and will go out of your way to contact me, even if it is inconvenient for you at the time.

Helpful Hints

1. Take time to think it through before you confront.

2. Use a sincere voice that expresses caring.

3. Be concrete and use specific examples.

4. Use one of the four primary feelings.

5. Make eye contact.

Helping Children With Feelings

Children need to know that expressing their feelings is OK. Parents need to learn how to help children express and handle their feelings of comfort and discomfort. The following steps are designed to encourage children to express their feelings.

1. **Label what you see or think you see.** If you don't see anything, guess and describe the feeling the child might have.

   - "You look really angry."

   - "You look so proud. Did something good happen?"

   - "I heard your friend is moving. You must feel really sad about that."

2. **Don't hog the conversation. Let the child do the talking.** It's hard for a child to follow his or her own train of thought if someone is interrupting, blaming, or giving advice, etc. Simply look interested in what the child is saying and listen.

3. **When your child wants something, honor the desire.** If you're in the grocery store and the child wants a toy, instead of just saying "NO!" try,

   - "Oh look, what a nice toy. Look at the colors. Wouldn't that be fun to have. I bet you would really like that toy. And you know what? I'd love to buy it for you if I could. But I only have enough money for food, dear."

   Or, if the child wants cookies or candy and you don't want him to have any, honor his desire to have the candy or cookies. You don't have to give in and buy the sweets — just honor the desire.

   - "Oh son, I know you really like those cookies and that they taste really good. If I could, dear, I'd buy you those cookies, but we can't afford anything other than fruit and milk."

   In this instance, you have honored his desire to eat the cookies but have explained why he can't have them.

   Another strategy is to give children choices by allowing them to pick between packages of cookies you approve of.

Your goal is to communicate with your child that you understand and value his desires and feelings. The process of honoring desires rather than saying "no" immediately shows children their opinions are valued.

"I know you want that sucker, but today we cannot buy it."

Personal Power

Personal power is the emotional capability we have to influence conditions in our lives which lead to meeting our needs. Personal power is not how physically strong we are—it is how emotionally strong we are. We can use our personal power in a positive way or negative, destructive way.

The use of our personal power in a positive sense means that we do things to meet our needs that build and strengthen our positive self-esteem and self-concept.

As nurturing parents, we use our personal power to help build a positive sense of self in our children. In turn, we want our children to use their own personal power to meet their own needs in a positive way. People who use their personal power in a positive way generally feel good about themselves as men and women.

Some people use their personal power in a negative way. That is, the things they do to get their needs met are destructive. Alcohol and drug dependency, fighting, stealing, cheating, or hitting are all ways people can use their personal power in a negative way.

People who use their personal power in a negative way generally feel bad about themselves as men and women. Our goal is to help people use their personal power in a positive way to reinforce positive self-concept and positive self-esteem.

To Develop a Sense of Personal Power in Yourself

- Take ownership of your feelings.
- Take responsibility for your own behavior.
- Make decisions to problems that will increase your sense of self-worth.
- Communicate using I statements.
- Praise yourself for being and doing.
- Follow through with commitments.
- Be aware of the needs and feelings of others.

To Develop a Sense of Personal Power in Your Children

- Treat children with respect and dignity.
- Praise your children for being and doing.
- Give children opportunities for success.
- Encourage your children to take responsibility for their feelings.
- Provide your children with choices and consequences.
- Listen and talk to your children.
- Respect your child's body.
- Be nurturing and consistent in helping children learn appropriate behaviors.

Control

Control is the use of your personal power to manage, dictate, and steer your own behavior — or another person's behavior and needs — for self gain.

Controlling another person's behavior is necessary when that person is unable to meet his/her own basic needs. Infants, elderly, disabled, mentally ill, and bedridden patients all require help in meeting their basic needs. In these instances, controlling a major part of a person's life is positive and appropriate.

Controlling an infant's behavior is OK.

Controlling another person's life when that person has the capability of managing his/her own behavior, or meeting his/her own needs is an inappropriate use of control. Not allowing children to take responsibility for their own behavior is using control in a negative way. Using control in a negative way leads to negative feelings. These negative feelings will only lead to rebellion, inadequate feelings of self, and extreme forms of dependency.

Spoiling Your Children

A spoiled child is a boy or girl who has learned to be defiant, demanding, and manipulative. Spoiled children do not respond well to limits placed on their behavior by their parents. They generally have a hard time waiting for things they want and will often respond with temper tantrums — hitting, breaking, or throwing things when told "no." It is important to recognize that children approximately one year and younger are never considered to be "spoiled." The developmental stage of infancy requires babies to demand their needs be met. As they grow older, their needs become less demanding.

How Do Children Become Spoiled?

Spoiling children is not an easy task. It takes a lot of time, effort, and attentiveness on the part of a parent to spoil a child. Spoiling children requires a parent to perform the following behaviors:

- Do everything for a child so he does nothing for himself.

- Anticipate a child's request so he never has to ask for anything.

- Spend all your waking hours together.

- Prohibit any type of short separation from the child; even having a babysitter.

- Only pick a child up when he cries.

- Be inconsistent in the limits and rules you set down so a child never knows what to expect.

- Blame the child for being demanding and demonstrate anger toward him.

If you follow the above steps, we guarante you will have a spoiled child.

"Where did we go wrong?"

Myths and Facts About Spoiling Children

Myth:

You will spoil your child by picking him up when he cries.

Fact:

If the only time you hold your child is when he cries, the child soon learns he has to cry to be held. Picking him up only when he cries is a good way to spoil a child. Make sure you spend twice as much time holding your child when he's not crying. The child will at least learn he doesn't have to cry to be held.

Myth:

Children who throw temper tantrums are spoiled.

Fact:

Temper tantrums are a way a young child expresses his frustration toward a situation or person. Young children are essentially very needy people; they want what they want now, not later. Setting reasonable limits helps children develop patience and delays in their need for gratification. Expect a few temper tantrums along the way and don't become too alarmed. Make sure you read the information on ignoring as a way of helping children learn other ways of expressing frustration.

Expect a few temper tantrums.

Myth:

A spoiled child is one who has not been spanked.

Fact:

Spanking a child never prevented one from becoming spoiled. The absence of reasonable limits and consequences for inappropriate behavior contributes to spoiling a child, not the absence of spanking. Spanking is a type of hitting; hitting is a type of hurting touch; hurting touch is a type of abuse. A nurturing parent uses other, more effective, means of discipline and punishment than hitting.

Myth:

A young child is incapable of doing anything for himself.

Fact:

Children can learn very early in life to participate in getting their own needs met. They can help in getting dressed, wiping their mouths after eating, feeding themselves, and brushing their teeth. Children enjoy doing things for themselves because they feel more powerful and more in control of their environment.

Myth:

If my child is spoiled, to cure him I have to become harsh and mean.

Fact:

If you find you have spoiled your child, here are some suggestions:

- If your child is too demanding and wants you to pick him up, explain that you have work to do and will hold him in a little while. Try redirecting him to a new activity.

- If your child wakes up once, or several times during the night wanting your company and entertainment, he has to learn there is nothing to be gained by waking and crying. It might mean letting the child cry 15 to 20 minutes the first few times without touching, talking, or even letting the child see you. Although it may seem like forever, the crying will soon subside.

- If your child has difficulty separating from you, try brief periods of being apart. You might first try inviting a babysitter over while you remain in the house so the child gets to feel comfortable with someone else. Then gradually go away for 5, 15, 25 minutes reassuring and praising the child when you return. Soon he will feel more secure and confident that you are not apt to abandon him.

Encourage Healthy Child Behaviors

No child is ever born spoiled. Becoming spoiled is a learned behavior like being afraid of the dark, or not liking to eat certain foods. Children learn to be spoiled from the people who serve as their primary caregivers.

- Help your child by helping yourself learn new, nurturing parenting attitudes and child rearing practices.

- Pay attention to the needs of your child without overdoing it.

- Promote independence by encouraging your child to do things for himself.

- Model for your child the proper way to handle disappointment, frustration, and sadness so he can act more appropriately.

The payoffs for encouraging healthy behavior in children last a lifetime!

Nurturing Ways to Handle Anger

Anger is a feeling of being irritated, disgusted, irked, annoyed, or furious. People get angry when they have been hurt. Everyone has angry feelings from time to time. Most of the anger people feel is not violent or difficult to control. Knowing how to handle your anger will model for your children an appropriate way to express their anger.

Feeling anger and expressing anger are healthy for everyone. There is nothing wrong with the feeling of anger. What gets a lot of people in trouble is how they express their anger. Taking anger out on someone else is never okay. Hitting, yelling, and belittling others are not appropriate ways of letting others know that you feel angry.

Listed below are ways of expressing your anger that help you get your feelings expressed without hurting someone else.

1. **Angry Letter**

   Write a short letter to each person you are angry with. Tell them that you are angry with them for what they did or didn't do. Put the letter in its own envelope and place it where you can easily see it. When you feel the anger again, open it up and read it. Add how you're feeling to the end of it. Keep the letter for a few weeks or as long as you feel relief when you look at it. After you no longer have the need to look at the letter, get rid of it. Dispose of the letter with a ceremony. Make it a meaningful occasion.

2. **Angry Cry and Scream**

   Close yourself in a room away from everyone. Scream out your worst opinion of this person. The louder you scream the better. It's okay if you begin to cry. When you're done, wash your hands and face and go for a walk.

3. **Anger Role Play**

   Imagine the person you're angry with is sitting across from you in an empty chair. Tell this person how angry you are with him/her. Then, move to the empty chair and speak as he/she would speak to you. Then jump back to your chair and discredit the person's argument and logic. Tear it to shreds. Go back and forth, playing yourself and the other person as long and as often as you need.

4. **Physical Exercise Activities**

   Go jogging, do sit-ups, run up and down a flight of stairs, exert yourself in exercise. When you begin feeling exhausted, do ten more — each time calling out the person's name in anger.

5. **Angry Shreds**

   Write the name of the person you're angry with in large letters on a piece of paper. Tear the paper into as many pieces as you can. The quicker you tear, the better. Burn the scraps or flush them in the toilet bowl. While you're doing this, think "You deserve my anger." It really works.

6. **Ridiculous Imagery**

   Exaggerate personal aspects of the person with whom you are angry. It could be their physical appearance, name, professional role, or profession.

Handling My Anger

Write down your responses to the following statements.

1. One situation that occurs at home that often results in my getting angry is _____

2. When I am angry, I am apt to _____

   When this occurs, I feel _____

   and those around me feel _____

3. One way I would like to handle my anger is _____

4. List three things I can do to handle my anger.

   a.

   b.

   c.

Reducing My Stress

Stress is the body's way of saying life and its situations are more than one can handle at the moment. Stress occurs when situations in life impact upon a person which overwhelm a person's capability to manage, cope, or deal with the situation. Change, loss, inappropriate expectations, demands, etc., are generally stress producing events.

Use the following techniques to reduce stress.

1. **Organize your day.** Organize your life's events in a way which makes life easier. Have an alternative baby sitter in case yours gets sick. Plan the next day's activities the night before. Make your child's lunch the night before and keep it in the refrigerator. Store related items; for example, cleaning supplies, rags, and vaccum cleaner in one location. When you have finished with them, return them to their proper place.

2. **Change your environment.** Sometimes too much change can produce stress. Sometimes change is necessary to reduce stress. A balance is obviously necessary. Some ways to create change is by rearranging your furniture, painting walls new colors, meeting new people, going to school, getting a different job, or getting a new haircut.

3. **Communicate your feelings.** Talking to others who care enough to listen is important in reducing stress. Sharing your thoughts, feelings, goals, frustrations, joys, and successes with people who listen reaffirms a personal sense of positiveness. It also provides us with a support system. Communication also means listening to others, like your children. They also experience stress when they feel they're not listened to. Listening to others is a way to build a support network. Another technique to reduce stress is to learn to say "no." Practice your assertiveness skills without being critical.

4. **Be your own best friend.** Work on building a positive regard for yourself. Nurture yourself. Take care of yourself. Eat properly, exercise, and learn relaxation skills. Avoid people and things that detract from your overall health. If you are sexually active, practice safe sex. Avoid drugs—they only harm you and your children. Being the best possible person you can be is the best insurance against becoming overwhelmed by stress.

5. **Choose friends who respect you.** Your friends play an important part in your life. Sometimes friends can be supportive of your effort to grow. Sometimes friends can suggest things to do that detract from growth rather than promote growth. Part of being your own best friend is to wisely choose friends who help you grow.

Reduce your stress for a happier, healthier life.

Why Parents Hit Their Children

For as long as anyone cares to remember, hitting has been used by parents and adults as a way of communicating their anger with children and their behaviors. Some say hitting children actually began thousands of years ago when cave people lived on the earth. Our image of cave parents running around with clubs hitting each other and their children on the head might be fairly accurate. Verbal language as a means of communication was slow in developing. Hitting was a way a cave mother said to her cave son, "I am not pleased with you, or what you did, or failed to do."

Hitting may actually have begun thousands of years ago.

Although parents today generally don't use clubs, the practice of hitting children is unfortunately still widely used. The most widely used type of hitting today is spanking. There are several common reasons why parents hit their children. Let's examine those reasons.

Parents Hit Children to Teach Them Right From Wrong

Hitting and spanking children often occurs because parents want their children to learn right from wrong. When children do something wrong, many parents feel a spanking will help them do the right thing rather than continue to do the wrong thing. Using the old theory of "When there's pain, there's gain," parents feel a "good spanking" will teach children not to misbehave. The reality is that spanking communicates to children that they not only did something wrong but they also are bad. In addition, hitting never teaches children what to do or what is the right thing to do. Instead it only teaches children what is wrong. Until children are taught what to do instead, misbehavior will continue.

Parents Hit Children as a Form of Punishment

For many parents, hitting is the only way they know how to punish children for misbehaving. Some view parents not hitting their children as a form of punishment as not using any form of punishment at all. It is a fear of the parents that children will be allowed to do what they want and will be out of control. Punishment, when used with rewards, is an effective way for teaching right from wrong. Punishments like time-out, being grounded, loss of privilege, paying for something purposely broken, and disappointment expressed by the parent are far more effective forms of punishment than hitting. In these instances, children learn that they are still OK people even though they misbehaved.

Parents Hit Children Based on Religious Writings

"Spare the rod, spoil the child" is the single most misquoted and misunderstood phrase in literature. Many people hit their children based on the belief that God sanctions violence toward children. Interpreted literally, the rod to many means a stick. If you spare hitting your child's body with a stick, not only will the child grow up spoiled, but also you've disobeyed the word of God. The actual verse that appears in the Bible is Proverbs 13:24. "He that spareth his rod, hateth his son; but he who loveth him, chasteneth him betimes." Many members of the clergy believe that the rod was actually the staff used by the shepherds to guide and tend their sheep. They used the curved, top part of the stick to guide, not hit sheep. Using a stick to hit children's bodies is only a justification parents use for their frustration and anger. Hitting is clearly an act of violence, not of love.

Parents Hit Children As an "Act of Love"

Many parents feel that hitting children is an act of "love" born out of a deep concern for their well-being. Parents who hit as an act of love tell their children how much they love them while they're hitting them. Statements like "If I didn't love you, I wouldn't be doing this"; "This hurts me more than it hurts you"; "One day you'll thank me for this"; or, "This is for your own good" send confusing messages. When children hear their mom and dad tell them how much they love them while they're getting hit and feeling hurt, children become confused. If such interactions continue throughout childhood, children learn that people who love them are also people who can hurt them. Far too many women choose husbands and boyfriends who show them love the same way dad did.

Hitting those you love sends confusing messages.

Parents Hit Children Because It's a Cultural Practice

Many believe that hitting children is a way for parents to express their cultural practice. Parents with black skin, white skin, brown skin, yellow skin, and red skin all believe hitting is unique to their culture. Hitting is so widespread throughout American society that hitting children is a societal belief rather than a cultural practice. Parents today feel that because great grandpa hit grandpa, and grandpa hit dad, and dad hit his children, a cultural practice developed. Most people today, regardless of culture or race, have been hit as children.

Parents Hit Children to Prepare Them for the Real World

Violence is widespread in our society. We see it on TV and in movies. We read about it in newspapers and magazines. We witness it in our neighborhoods. Because violence is so common, many parents believe they need to prepare their child for the violence-filled "real world" by "toughening them up." So, parents hit children at home to prepare them for the violent world they live in.

The reality is that the "real world" for a developing boy or girl is not outside his/her home, but within. What goes on within the home teaches and prepares children to handle the "outside world." Violence in the home is transmitted to the neighborhood. Children learn to behave with others the way they were treated at home. The "real world" would become less violent if violence in the home stopped.

Why Shouldn't I Hit My Child?

Hitting teaches something other than obeying rules and being careful. Hitting teaches children fear, poor self-concept, revenge, and permission to hit those you love.

Hitting, even the threat of hitting, often teaches children fear. Children who learn to fear their parents often learn to fear other adults as well. Just the sheer differences in physical size between parents and children can be frightening. When parents threaten or use their physical superiority as a form of punishment, young children realize there is no way they could ever win. Their safety is literally at the mercy of the angry parent.

The self-concept and self-esteem of children develop from how they are treated. Children who are constantly threatened or hit learn that they are not worthy people, are not loved, and are not wanted. Nobody ever feels good after being hit. The more frequent the hitting, the more constant the feelings of inadequacy.

Children who have been repeatedly hit want to seek revenge. Getting back is a common result of spanking. Young children who can't hit back may seek to get revenge in other ways. Breaking something that belongs to the parents, writing on the walls, or stealing are some ways children can "get back at" the person who is hitting. The idea of learning the appropriate behavior, or of being good, takes a back seat to feelings of revenge.

Children may try to "get back at" the person who is hitting.

Parents who hit children risk teaching children that hitting those you love is okay. In this way, children learn that hitting is permissible and acceptable. Statements like "Mommy loves you and is doing this for your own good," or "Daddy loves you very much and this going to hurt me more than it will hurt you," confuses children and sends double messages. Such confusion is carried over years later when children who were constantly spanked become parents and use the same practice on their children. We know that child abuse is often passed on from parents to children like a family heirloom.

Myths and Facts About the Value of Spanking

Myth:

Children who aren't spanked become spoiled.

Fact:

Spoiled children are those who constantly want their own way. They choose not to listen to parents and are unaware of the needs of others. Children learn such behaviors, they are not the result of not spanking. Such behaviors result from inconsistent parenting, failure to provide necessary structure, and neglect of children's needs. Spanking children to prevent them from becoming spoiled is only a myth. Being sensitive to the needs of children in a consistent, loving, nurturing way is the best means available to prevent children from becoming spoiled.

Myth:

Only spank children when you are not angry.

Fact:

Such a statement is made to prevent parents from becoming too severe with their spanking. Some parents can't control their anger and feel that once they begin hitting their children, they won't be able to stop. The thought here is if children deserve to be punished, wait until you have calmed down before you spank. If you are not angry and have calmed down, why spank at all? You are in control. Talk to your children and let them know you are angry. Use other forms of punishment you are learning in this program that are much more effective. Use punishments such as time-out or loss of privilege. You will feel better about the punishment and so will your children. What's more, managing their behavior will become a lot easier.

Myth:

An occasional spanking is good for children.

Fact:

The word good indicates something good is happening to the children. An occasional spanking cannot help children learn behaviors parents feel are desirable. Being hit never feels good. Hitting has no long-term value.

Being spanked or hit does not feel good and has no benefit.

Myth:

Spanking your children is the only way to let them know you're angry.

Fact:

Parents often relieve their stress and frustration by hitting their children when they are angry with them. Although letting off steam is good for the parent, there is no value in the spanking for the children.

Myth:

Infants need to be spanked because they can't understand the language.

Fact:

Hitting an infant is always a dangerous practice. The physical development of a young infant is too fragile to withstand any force. Infants can't communicate verbally. This does not mean they can't learn. Infants learn from the touch, facial expressions, and tone of voice of the parents. A firm "no" spoken to an infant who is about to reach for a valued object is better than slapping the infant's hands. The "no" communicates your dislike of the behavior; the slap communicates your dislike of the infant.

A firm NO communicates your dislike of an infant's behavior.

Myth:

Children deserve to be spanked.

Fact:

Nobody every deserves to be hit. The skills you are learning in this program will help you replace spanking with more beneficial and pleasant ways of managing the behaviors of your children.

Discipline, Rewards, and Punishment

Helping children learn right from wrong and good from bad is one of the primary responsibilities of parents. Despite what many parents feel, children really want to please their parents out of genuine love and respect. Children also know that their parents are the primary source of their love, fun, games, food, and shelter. Just like anyone else, children know a good thing when they see one.

Children are also curious. They are like explorers in diapers. They want to touch things that look like fun. Since a baby's mouth is his or her primary way of testing things out, babies are constantly putting things into their mouths. They really don't know the difference between good or bad. Children don't know what is dangerous and what isn't. Their minds haven't developed enough yet to know good from bad.

Young children also operate on the "gimme" principle. "Gimme, gimme, gimme now, right now," is a common feeling expressed by children. They can't help it. That's just the way God made little boys and little girls. As children grow older, they learn to wait and have patience.

Knowing how young children operate is important for helping them learn how to manage their needs, desires, and behaviors. It also helps them grow up feeling good about themselves and others. Since practically every parent wants a good life for his/her child, parents need to learn about three ideas: discipline, rewards, and punishment.

What is Discipline?

Discipline comes from the word disciple. A disciple is a person who learned from his or her leader. A disciple of someone is a follower of the person's ideas, beliefs, and values. In this context, the word discipline means guidance — to guide another person in helping him/her learn right from wrong, good from bad.

Discipline also means boundaries and rules. For our purpose, discipline means family rules. Family rules are guidelines everyone in the family follows. Knowing what to do and what not to do helps children develop a sense of competence. It provides them with the ability to please their mom and dad.

In our program, discipline means family rules for everyone.

What is Punishment?

Punishment is a negative consequence for doing or not doing something. The purpose of punishment is to decrease the likelihood that bad behavior will occur again. The purpose of punishment is not to hurt children. Corporal punishment, like spanking, slapping, punching, etc., is a negative consequence that hurts children. It encourages them to grow up feeling lousy about themselves and others. The Nurturing Program philosophy of raising children supports a non-violent, caring way of rearing children. Punishment is a necessary part of discipline — helping children learn right from wrong. Hitting children's bodies, with your hand or with an object, is never okay and should never be practiced. Other techniques such as time-out, loss of privilege, and being grounded are far more effective in helping children learn.

Use appropriate behavior management techniques.

What are Rewards?

Rewards are positive consequences for doing the right thing and for following the family rules. The purpose of rewards is to reinforce the good behavior. Rewards let the other person know how pleased you are with his/her behavior or their presence. Rewards are a necessary and an important part in helping children learn right form wrong. Praise, good touch, and objects tell children you appreciate their efforts in doing good things. Families who use punishment, not rewards, only pay attention to children when they mess up. Everyone, including children, wants recognition. If the only time you pay attention to children is when they're doing something bad, they will continue to do bad things to get parents to recognize them.

Discipline, punishment, and rewards are all necessary for helping children grow up feeling good about themselves and good about others.

Verbal and Physical Redirection

Redirection is a technique designed especially for young preschool children that encourages them to perform desirable behaviors. Redirection is used by parents to prevent personal injury, promote desirable behavior, reduce punishing interactions, and promote learning and exploration.

Verbal Redirection

Verbal redirection is a means of managing your child's behavior by verbally expressing a command or request. It is a way to redirect the behavior of your child by talking to him. Verbal redirection is a parent initially telling a child that the behavior that is occurring, or about to occur, is not acceptable. A statement telling the child what is acceptable follows.

Appropriate Examples:

- "Chairs are for sitting. No standing, please."

- "No standing in the tubby. Sit, please."

- "Oh what a nice toy. Put it back on the shelf, please."

Inappropriate Examples:

- "No standing on the chair. You'll fall and break your neck."

- "Quit standing in the tub. What do you want, an accident?"

- "Yes, I see your toy. Now just don't leave it on the floor."

From the examples, the appropriate use of verbal redirection helps the child know what the parent expects and doesn't expect. The inappropriate use of verbal redirection actually doesn't redirect a child's behavior at all. Threats, statements of doom, and telling a child what not to do are not the correct ways to use verbal redirection.

Verbal redirection also includes directing the child's attention and behavior to appropriate activities and avoiding unnecessary confrontations.

Example:

Adam is about to run out of the bedroom when mom is trying to finish dressing him. She calls out "Adam, close the door for mom, please." Adam's attention is redirected from running away and he ends up complying and feeling like a helper.

This type of redirection works well with toddlers who haven't yet figured out that they are being redirected. It is not as effective after the age of three years.

"Let's play with the rattle instead of the socket."

Physical Redirection

Physical redirection is similar to verbal redirection with one more step. As you are verbally redirecting a child, you are physically redirecting him as well. In the correct use of physical redirection, parents are using nurturing touch to redirect the child to perform more appropriate behavior. A hand gently placed on the child's back or object taken from a child's grasp are some ways parents use physical redirection. Redirecting a hand from a dangerous object is another way to physically redirect.

Appropriate Examples:

- Physically redirecting a child away from an electric socket to a safe toy to play with.

- Escorting a child from the bathroom to the living room and engaging the child in play.

- Taking a dangerous object away from a child and substituting it with a safer one.

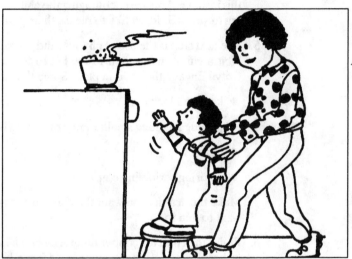

Use nurturing touch to physically redirect a child.

Inappropriate Examples:

- Physically jerking a child away from the electric socket.

- Spanking a child for entering the bathroom unassisted.

- Slapping a child's hand for touching a dangerous object.

In the appropriate use of physical redirection, a parent is using nurturing touch. In the inappropriate use of physical redirection, harsh and abusive touch is being used. The young preschool child is unable to make the connection between the harsh physical touch administered by the parent, and the danger to the object being touched. In the Nurturing Program, we believe the use of hitting, slapping, spanking, and other forms of harsh touch is abusive. Abusive touch has no positive value in helping a child learn appropriate behaviors.

Verbal and Physical Redirection Used Together

The ideal way to redirect a child's behavior is through the combined use of verbal and physical redirection. Used together, the child quickly learns that a particular behavior is unacceptable to his parents.

How to Use Verbal and Physical Redirection

Use the following steps to verbally and physically redirect your child:

1. In a firm voice, let the child know he is performing or about to perform an unacceptable behavior. The firm voice indicates this is not a game; the NO indicates he is to stop the behavior immediately.

2. Approach the child, stoop down, make eye contact, and hold his hands.

3. Tell the child his behavior is unacceptable. Use words like "icky," "ouch," or "hot" if he is near something that could injure him like an electric socket or hot oven. Use other words if the child has something in his hand or is touching something you prefer him not touching. Words like "No," "This is Mommy's; not for Billy," or "Sorry, this is not for little boys," convey the message. Used consistently, a child will begin to associate these words with certain behaviors.

4. Attempt to let the child re-establish the original setting. That is, if he has taken something, physically and verbally redirect him to return the object to where it belongs. If he has turned on an appliance, have him turn the appliance off. In this instance, you are encouraging the child to perform behaviors that are pleasing to you. Children like to please their parents.

5. The next step is the use of physical and verbal redirection. The goal is not to inhibit a child's natural curiosity, but to foster it through more appropriate activity. Engage the child in play. Some things young children like are:

   - keys and locks

   - putting anything smaller into something bigger

   - puzzles

   - coloring/scribbling on paper

   Make the activity you want the child to engage in so exciting that the child will want to join in.

6. Praise the child for cooperating. Tell him he is a good listener. Praise for doing will reinforce future encounters. After all, you want your child to listen and cooperate.

7. If the child chooses to perform the inappropriate behavior again, repeat steps one through six. A child is likely to repeat the behavior for two reasons: young children are too young to remember what was bad or good; and, some preschool children are likely to test you and the rule for consistency.

8. Physical redirection is usually necessary and is more effective with younger children when their language is not as well developed. Use physical redirection with some form of verbal redirection. Use physical redirection less as children get older, understand language better, and want to be independent.

"What a good listener you are. Thank you for listening."

Additional Advice:

Listed below are additional suggestions on how to use verbal and physical redirection.

1. **Never hit or spank a child as a means of physical redirection.** Hitting is an abusive practice that sends a double message: I'm concerned about your safety, but I hit you and cause you pain and fear.

2. **Save "No" for the big things.** Because toddlers like to explore, their whole world can become one big "No-No" if you let it. When you do use the word "No," show an expression of disapproval. Slowly turning the head from side to side (physical indicator of No) and a cold, non-smiling face tells the child you are displeased. After a while, just shaking your head "No" gets the message across.

3. **Baby proof your house.** Get all the valued objects, stereos, tape decks, statues, cassette tapes, etc. above your child's grasp level. Life will be easier for you and your child.

4. **Practice verbal and physical redirection.** If your child continues to want to perform the unacceptable behavior despite your efforts, it may be necessary to take the child to another room, or to spend more time with the child "to take his mind off whatever he wanted to touch."

5. **Finally, be consistent.** A "No" is a "No" every time the unacceptable behavior appears. If you're inconsistent in the application of your redirection, expect your child to be the same. Spend the time and energy now in being consistent. You and your child will find living together an enjoyable experience.

Family Rules

Family rules are the single most important part of helping children learn right from wrong. They teach children what is acceptable behavior to mom and dad, and what is not. Children will begin to understand the idea of rules around two years of age and will enjoy helping in developing the family rules.

The purpose of family rules is for parents and children to establish consistent guidelines that will help everyone know what is expected and what isn't expected. Family rules encourage family members to take responsibility for their own behavior. When children can talk and know the difference between right and wrong, family rules will help them, as well as their parents, get along better as a family.

Family rules are important because both parents and children have rights. Just like adults, children have the right to be listened to, to state their views, to be treated with respect, and to live in a world free from violence. Family rules help ensure that everyone in the family has equal rights and input into how the family operates.

Family rules are for everyone in the family. Often parents believe that children need rules but parents don't. Children quickly see the injustice when parents are able to do something, but children get punished for the same action. Comments like "That's not fair," or "How come you can do it and I can't?" are legitimate concerns. Parents, knowing the injustice exists but are unable to explain why, give such silly answers as "Because I said so," or "Because I'm you're mother (father)," or "Because."

Family rules are for everyone in the family.

Parents who seek complete control over their children and inappropriately desire them not to experiment or "always do as they're told" usually describe their wishes by stating "As long as you live under my roof, you obey my rules. If you think you can do better than me, pack up your things and get the hell out of my house." Such statements only reflect the parents' inadequacy and authoritarian feelings. Children learn not to think for themselves, not to take responsiblity for their behavior, and blame others for their mistakes.

Family Rules for Young Children

It's always a good idea to have family rules. However, infants are too young to follow the rules and should not be held responsible for complying with the rules. Children can begin to follow family rules when they: understand the difference between good and bad; verbally use words to express how they think and feel; and, can contribute in establishing the rules. Generally, most children around two years of age are capable of following family rules.

How to Establish Family Rules

There are seven easy steps to follow when establishing rules for your family.

1. **Get everyone to participate.** Have all family members sit around the kitchen table. Begin by suggesting that as long as everyone lives under one roof, they might as well have rules that apply to everyone. Have young children sit on laps or be present even if they can't contribute in identifying family rules.

2. **Share problem behaviors.** Encourage family members to share behaviors they feel are a problem. Talk freely about issues the family has to work on. Avoid blaming statements and fault finding.

3. **Brainstorm a list of rules wanted.** Use the worksheet on page 72 entitled **Establishing Family Rules.** Identify issues that you would like to have for a family rule. For every bahavior you don't want to see, identify a behavior you would like to have instead. Only stating the behaviors you don't want doesn't let children know the behaviors that you do want. Fill out both sides: What To Do and What Not To Do.

4. **Keep the rules simple and specific.** Be specific in wording your rules. A rule like "No running in the house" is too vague. What if there is a fire — certainly everyone should run out of the house. Be specific. If your children are playing a game that requires running, make it a family rule: No playing _(insert game)_ in house (what not to do). Play _(insert game)_ in yard (what to do). Remember — for every "what not to do," there has to be a "what to do." This way you're substituting what you want for what you don't want.

5. **Identify a consequence and reward for each rule.** For the rules to mean anything, a consequence must be associated with the rule. That is, when children choose to misbehave, a punishment must follow. When children choose to behave by following the rules, a reward must follow. Punishments and rewards tell the children that the rules have some meaning. Rewards and punishments are identified elsewhere in this Handbook.

6. **Limit Family Rules to a maximum of five.** Five rules are plenty. Keeping a short list of rules will help children remember the rules and practice them.

7. **Drop and add new rules when needed.** Rules are not written in concrete. When a behavior is no longer a problem, have a rule dropping party. Since the behavior has become part of the family operation, there is no need to have it in the list. It's not saying the rule is no longer important. The rule is not needed anymore because the behavior is no longer a problem. When new problem behaviors appear, have a family meeting and repeat steps 1-6.

Establishing Family Rules

Brainstorm a list of four or five possible family rules.

What To Do

1. _____

   _____

   Reward _____

2. _____

   _____

   Reward _____

3. _____

   _____

   Reward _____

4. _____

   _____

   Reward _____

5. _____

   _____

   Reward _____

What Not To Do

1. _____

   _____

   Penalty _____

2. _____

   _____

   Penalty _____

3. _____

   _____

   Penalty _____

4. _____

   _____

   Penalty _____

5. _____

   _____

   Penalty _____

Rules For The _____ Family

What To Do	**What Not To Do**

What To Do

1. _____
   _____

   Reward _____

2. _____
   _____

   Reward _____

3. _____
   _____

   Reward _____

4. _____
   _____

   Reward _____

5. _____
   _____

   Reward _____

What Not To Do

1. _____
   _____

   Penalty _____

2. _____
   _____

   Penalty _____

3. _____
   _____

   Penalty _____

4. _____
   _____

   Penalty _____

5. _____
   _____

   Penalty _____

Children Deserve Rewards

Rewards are the single most powerful means of helping children learn to behave appropriately. Rewards help children develop a positive self-esteem and a positive self-concept by communicating who they are and what they do are important. Children will do more for a reward than they will avoid doing out of fear of punishment.

Rewards are very powerful in motivating children. Use the following types of rewards to help children feel good about themselves and learn appropriate behaviors.

Praise

Praise is the single most powerful reward a child, or anyone, can receive. Use praise for being (I love you; you're a great daughter) and praise for doing (what a great job washing the car; good effort in buttoning your shirt) two to three times each day with each child. Don't forget — praise yourself each day.

Nurturing Touch

There are three types of touch: hurting, scary, and nurturing. Each of us has a personal touch history which includes all three types of touch. Gentle hugs, back rubs, soft strokes of a child's back with gentle rocking are all nice, positive types of nurturing touch. Everyone wants recognition. Nurturing touch is a nice way to let children know you value them. Use nurturing touch with praise. Together they make a powerful combination.

Privileges

Privileges serve as excellent rewards for children. A privilege can be extra TV time, getting to stay up past curfew, getting a few extra stories read at night, or other behaviors your children enjoy. Privileges should never include basic needs the child has such as stimulation, time with parents, security, love, or trust.

Objects

Some parents like to reward their children with various objects in addition to praise and touch. Objects can include almost anything that ranges from stickers to assorted toys. Find out what your child likes and occasionally reward him or her with an object.

Allowance

When children get older, paying them an allowance for chores they have completed is an excellent way to reward them. Allowance in the form of money teaches children how to be responsible and manage money. With the child, decide on the amount of money and a plan for its management.

There is no such thing as recognizing too much good in children. Remember the rule to encourage children to behave: What you pay attention to is what you get more of. Pay more attention to the good things children do. You will then get more of the good things.

Punishing Behavior

Punishment is a necessary part of helping children learn right from wrong, good from bad. Rewards are consequences for following the family rules and behaving appropriately, punishment is the consequence for breaking the rules and misbehaving. The philosophy of the Nurturing Program is that hitting children and/or yelling at them are not acceptable forms of punishment. Hitting and yelling teach children they're no good. We're interested in teaching children that they're good people, although what they did was wrong.

Never Punish Infants

There are six very important reasons why you should never punish an infant:

- Infants do not understand cause and effect (if something happens, something else will happen).

- Infants do not perform misdeeds or misbehavior on purpose. They are only exploring their environment and need protection from being hurt.

- Baby-proofing, redirection, and praise are three good strategies to use in helping infants manage their environment.

- Infants do not have the cognitive skills to know the difference between right and wrong.

- Infants need love, protection, and support — not punishment.

- If you become frustrated with what your infant is doing, rather than punish the infant, find a quiet place to calm down.

Infants need love, protection, and support — not punishment.

Type of Punishments

There are four types of punishments that are appropriate for young children ages 2 1/2 to 5 years.

- **Loss of Privilege:** Appropriate for 2 1/2 years and older. A privilege is a right granted by the parent. Privileges can be watching TV, playing with a certain toy in the house, etc. If a child misuses the object or misuses the privilege, he/she loses it for awhile. Take away a toy or a privilege only when the child misuses it (thrown, broken, etc.).

- **Being Grounded:** Appropriate for child 3 1/2 years and older. When a child leaves a yard or an area purposely, without permission, an appropriate punishment is being grounded to the yard or house. The child must know it wasn't appropriate to leave the yard. If the child does not understand the behavior was inappropriate, do not use grounding as a punishment.

- **Parental Disappointment:** Appropriate for child 2 1/2 years and older. Parental disappointment is a simple statement which expresses the disappointment a parent has in a behavior the child has chosen to perform. The intent is to build some caring and an awareness in the child of the parent's disappointment. An example of the use of parental disappointment is: "Son, I want you to know how disappointed I am that you chose to hit your brother (or whatever the misdeed). I'm sure the next time you're upset, you won't hit your brother and you will tell him not to take your toys. But right now, I feel disappointed." Follow this statement telling the child he is either grounded or has to take a time-out.

- **Time-Out:** Appropriate for child 3 years and older. Time-out is a temporary isolation of the child from others because he/she chose to act inappropriately. It is a technique that lets children know that when they choose to be mean to others, they will have to be by themselves for awhile sitting quietly. Time-out is not isolating a child for a long time. It is not solitary confinement in some dark room. It is not a threat of the loss of a parent's love or protection. Time-out is a temporary isolation of the child from others because he/she chose to act inappropriately. It is a technique that lets children know that when they choose to violate a rule, they will have to sit quietly by themselves for awhile.

When To Use Time-Out

Use time-out when the child has seriously violated one or more of the family rules. Some examples may be:

- deliberately breaking something

- throwing objects in the house

- ignoring a request to stop doing something

- abusive behaviors to others such as hitting, kicking, swearing, or pulling hair.

When Not To Use Time-Out

Do not use time-out for minor infractions of family rules, for behaviors you find partially annoying or unacceptable, or for normal accidents. Try ignoring the behavior or use another form of behavior management instead of time-out. The selected use of time-out will increase its effectiveness as a management technique.

Before You Use Time-Out

1. **Make sure the child understands the concept of time-out.** Before using time-out as a form of punishment, make sure the child understands what time-out is and what you expect once he/she is in time-out. Using time-out before the child completely understands the concept is unfair and will only cause the child confusion.

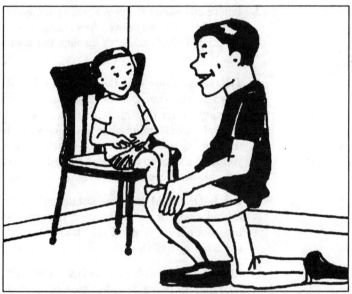

Explain time-out and make sure your child understands it.

2. **Establish rules that will warrant a time-out.** These should be family rules that all family members obey. If abusive behavior to others is not allowed in the house, this means both children and parents should not be abusive. If silliness at the dinner table is not acceptable then everyone has to sit appropriately and eat the meal. It is important that parents follow the rules themselves, otherwise children will find the rules unjust. Modeling appropriate behavior is the best way to help a child manage his or her own behavior.

3. **Pick a time-out place.** The area should be without interesting things to do or look at. Sending a child to his/her bedroom would not be an appropriate time-out. A child's bedroom has too many things to do (read, color, play) or look at (television, magazines, pictures). A stairway (for children who can walk), hallway, behind a door, or a chair facing the wall are all appropriate possibilities for a time-out place. There's not much to do at these places except sit and wait. **NEVER** lock a child in a room, or use a dark scary room, or rooms without enough air ventilation for time-out. Time-out is the removal of a child from a pleasant situation to a non-reinforcing situation. It is not a jail sentence.

4. **Establish how long the time-out will last.** The precise amount of time depends on the age of the child and the seriousness of the offense. Less serious behaviors get one to two minutes of time-out; more serious behaviors get three to seven minutes. Short duration time-outs (1-7 minutes) are more effective than longer time-outs (15-30 minutes).

How To Use Time-Out

1. **Give the child one warning that the behavior is inappropriate and if it continues, he or she will have to take a time-out.** For example, you might say, "Tom, silliness is not acceptable at the dinner table. If you continue to act silly, you will have to leave the dinner table and take a two-minute time-out."

2. **If inappropriate behavior continues, tell the child to go to the time-out area.** If the child resists leaving, use minimum physical force to ensure the departure to time-out. Accomplish departure to time-out by gently, but firmly, taking a child by his or her arm, or under both arms near the shoulder and encouraging the child to take the time-out. Never use abusive physical force to accomplish a time-out. The consequence of the inappropriate behavior is lost in the abuse force.

3. **Ignore all comments, promises, or arguments by the child that she or he won't do the behavior anymore.** Any attention by the parent may reinforce the inappropriate behavior. Carry through the command to have the child take a time-out.

4. **Tell the child how long the time-out will last.** Be very specific. "Tom, you have a two-minute time-out for acting silly at the dinner table after I gave you one warning. After two minutes of sitting quietly, you may return." It is not up to the child to determine when to return, or up to you to decide when you can stand the child again. Time-out is a formal consequence to a formal family rule. If you have a kitchen timer, it is a good way to be accurate and to make the time-out objective. Remember to ignore any inquiries about when time-out is over.

5. **Remind the child that time-out doesn't start until he or she is quiet.** If the child is loud, cries, or runs away from the time-out place, take the child back to the time-out place. Remind the child that the time-out period begins when he or she is sitting quietly.

6. **After the time-out is over, redirect the child to appropriate behaviors.** Praise the child for being quiet in time-out. If you had to remove the child from the dinner table, allow the child to finish dinner. If the inappropriate behavior occurred during play time, spend a little time with the child modeling appropriate behavior for the play activity. If the inappropriate behavior occurs again, time-out must be readministered.

Some Points To Consider

Time-out works best with pre-school and school age children. Time-out with teenagers is not a useful behavior management technique. Other management techniques such as choices and consequences and loss of privileges are more effective with adolescents.

Time-out can be voluntary or involuntary. A child can initiate voluntary time-out after an inappropriate behavior has taken place. Involuntary time-out is when the parent requests that the child leave the area after some misdeed.

Helping Children Manage Their Behavior

Giving Children Choices

Giving choices is the most powerful way of building personal power in children. Children, like teens, want to feel powerful. Power, for most, is the ability to influence some aspects of your life by choice. Saying no, refusing to go to bed, or not taking a bath are some of the ways children exert their power. Temper tantrums are another way children exert their power. To help children utilize their power in a positive way, give them choices to make decisions on parts of their lives they view as important. Children will feel more powerful and use their power in a positive way because choices:

- provide a good way for children to use their power.

- help children learn to manage their own behavior.

- let children know they have power.

- are a good way to defuse potential power struggles.

- help children take responsibility for their behavior.

Giving children choices can begin at birth. The following are some areas where choices can be given:

- **Dressing:** "Son, what shirt would you like to wear—your blue one or your green one?"

- **Eating:** "Amy, would you like to drink your milk in a red cup or in a white cup?"

- **Bath Time:** "Larry, do you want to play first and then take a bath, or take a bath first?"

- **Play Time:** "Do you want to ride your tricycle or play in the sandbox?"

"Michelle, do you want to wear your skirt or a dress today?"

Choices and Consequences

Providing children choices for their behavior and consequences for those choices is an excellent technique to help children manage their own behavior. When using choices and consequences, first state the options children have and then the consequences for each of those options. Some examples are:

- "Children, you can either play nicely together and share your toys, or both of you will have to take a quiet time-out."

- "Mary, I expect you to quietly eat your dinner at the table. If you continue to act silly, you will have to leave the table. It's your choice."

"You can share the toys, or I will put them on the shelf."

Some important points to remember when using choices and consequences:

- **Never use threats as choices.** Parents either can't carry them through or don't want to. (Example — "If you don't leave your sister alone, I'm gonna break your neck!")

- **Never give ultimatums as choices.** (Example — "I'll never talk to you again if you don't shut up!") Ultimatums can rarely be carried through and soon children learn your words are hot air.

- **Never give choices when there aren't any.** (Example — "Son, would you like to get your coat on now. We have to go!") If the child answers "no," but he really has to get his coat on anyway, he never really had a choice.

Consequences must be related to the behavior you wish to increase or decrease.

Problem Solving and Decision Making

Problem solving is what you do when you know you have a problem but do not know what to do.

Decision making is what you do when you know what your alternatives are.

Another technique to help children use their power and take responsibility for their behavior is through a process called problem solving. Problem solving is useful when choices don't work or the child refuses to cooperate. Problem solving helps children learn what to do to resolve problems. Children learn to become independent thinkers, take responsibility for their behavior, and gain a sense of mastery over their environment.

The problem solving process is accomplished by following the seven steps listed below:

1. **Identify the problem.** Write the problem down in a full sentence. Be specific. Vague problems cannot be solved — only specific ones. If there is more than one problem, work on only one at a time. Some examples of problems could be:

   - "I don't have enough money."

   - "My daughter won't go to bed on time."

   - "I don't like a messy house."

   - "My children don't like taking baths."

   - "My relationships aren't good."

   - "I don't feel fulfilled."

2. **Determine who owns the problem.** Is it your problem, or is it your child's problem? Is your child doing something you do not approve of but does not see the behavior as a problem? A problem will continue as long as the people involved do not view it as a problem. Sit with your child and say, "Son, we have a problem. The problem is _____ .

"We have a problem. The problem is you don't like baths."

3. **Discuss what you have tried.** Talk with the person involved with the problem and review past efforts on solving the problem. Remember to use I statements rather than blaming you messages.

4. **What would you like to see instead?** This step allows everyone to look forward to resolving the problem by substituting the problem behavior with another behavior. Using the phrase "how to" as a beginning is suggestive and helpful.

   ● "How to have enough money."

   ● "How to help my daughter go to bed on time."

   ● "How to have a clean house."

   ● "How to help my children enjoy bath time."

   ● "How to have good relationships."

   ● "How to make myself feel fulfilled."

   This is the hardest step because you have to be very clear about what you want. There is a big difference between having enough money and making more money. You might have enough money if you learn how to live on less and that might make you happier than if you had set making more money as a goal and then had to get another job.

5. **List as many ways as you can to achieve what you would like to see instead.** Ask friends for ideas and think of other creative ideas. This is an individual brainstorming process and you should let yourself be as wild and funny as you can because it might trigger other ideas or help you to look at your possible solutions in a new way. Work with your family in identifying solutions to the problem.

"I could wash the windows, put things away, dust, ..."

6. **Pick out your three favorite ideas from step five.** Decide on ways you will try to solve the problem. As a family, decide on things together. Negotiate and compromise with your family.

7. **Try your new ideas.** If they do not work, repeat the process beginning with step one. The problem may be different than you originally thought.

Try your new ideas to achieve your goal.

Problem Solving and Decision Making Worksheet

1. Identify the problem:

   _____

2. Who owns the problem?

   _____

3. What have you tried?

   _____

4. What would you like to see instead?

   _____

5. How can you achieve what you would like to see?

   a. _____

   b. _____

   c. _____

   d. _____

   e. _____

   f. _____

6. Pick out your three favorite ideas from step five.

7. Try your new ideas. If the problem remains, go back to step one to see if your have identified the problem correctly. Repeat steps 2-7.

Negotiation and Compromise

The last technique to encourage children to express their power appropriately is through negotiation and compromise.

Every parent and child has at some time disagreed on which clothes to wear, what food to eat, when to go to bed, etc. Not always agreeing on things is normal. Children have their views, feelings, and opinions—so do parents. Parents expect things to be done a certain way—so do children. A nurturing family will attempt to work out their differences—not fight over them. In just about all cases, both the children and parents are never completely right all the time. Both views are valid simply because they belong to the people who state them.

There is no magic cure to getting everyone to agree on everything all the time. There is a way of trying to achieve a solution to opposing views. The process is called negotiation. Negotiation is used successfully in many situations. Differences between management and their employees, athletes and team owners, and heads of state from different nations agreeing to the terms of a peace treaty, are just some of the many instances negotiation is utilized as a process for helping resolve differences.

Negotiation can be used to resolve differences between parents and children. Let us look at the following steps to see how negotiation works:

1. When asking for something or stating a view, first determine if there is a difference of opinion between you and your children.

2. State your views and what you think the views of your children are. Remember to be confrontive, not critical, and to use I statements, not blaming you messages.

3. Ask your children if your impression of the problem and your understanding of their views are accurate. Listen openly to their views. Do not walk away, or argue, but listen. Remember, their views are equally as valid as yours.

4. Offer a compromise. Be sure to take into account their views as well as your own. Keep negotiating until an agreement is reached.

5. Offer choices. People like to feel they have options. "You can have juice or milk to drink before supper."

Use negotiation to communicate.

Facts About AIDS

AIDS is the abbreviation for Acquired Immune Deficiency Syndrome, which results from a viral infection and most often causes death. The AIDS virus does its damage by breaking down the body's shield against disease, its immune system. Because they have lost this natural shield against disease, people with AIDS get diseases that usually do not seriously harm those whose immune systems are working. These diseases take advantage of weakened immune systems and are called opportunistic diseases. Some of the opportunistic diseases that occur most often in people with AIDS are:

- Kaposi's sarcoma, a kind of skin cancer

- pneumocystic carinii, a kind of pneumonia

- toxoplasmosis, a parasite that can infect the brain and the central nervous system, and that can cause pneumonia

- crytosporidiosis, an intestinal parasite that causes extreme diarrhea

- candidiasis, a fungus that coats the intestinal tract and is seen most often in the inside of the throat as hard, white patches of growth

- cytomegalovirus (CMV), a viral infection of the digestive tract

- herpes simplex, a virus causing the ulceration of mucous membranes as well as of the digestive and circulatory systems

- lymphoma, a cancer which, in AIDS, affects the brain

- cryptococcal meningitis

What Causes AIDS?

The AIDS virus, recently renamed HIV (human immunodeficiency virus), is a newly discovered kind of virus called a retrovirus. Retroviruses are difficult for scientists to understand because they continually develop new structures. The ability of retroviruses to change structure also complicates the development of medical treatment for AIDS and frustrates the search for a vaccine to prevent it. It is not yet known whether the HIV virus is the direct cause of AIDS or if its ability to produce an AIDS infection results from a damaged immune system. One or both of these possibilities may be true.

Scientists do not know why most people exposed to the AIDS virus have not developed symptoms. In fact, they suppose that the majority of them may never develop symptoms. They believe, however, that those who have no symptoms, who are asymptomatic, may carry the virus for many years following their exposure to it.

Other people who are exposed to the AIDS virus and who do not develop full-blown cases of AIDS, may develop a less life-threatening condition called AIDS-Related Complex (ARC).

How is AIDS Spread?

The AIDS virus does not survive easily outside the human body, and it is not transmitted through air, food, or water. People can only contract the virus by having certain bodily fluids (blood or semen) that are contaminated with the virus come into contact with their own bloodstreams.

What are the Symptoms of AIDS?

Symptoms of the opportunistic diseases associated with AIDS may include:

- swelling or hardening of glands located in the throat, groin, or armpit

- the appearance of hard, discolored or purplish growths on the skin or inside the mouth

- the appearance of a thick, whitish coating on the tongue or mouth, called "thrush," which may also be accompanied by a sore throat

- increasing shortness of breath

- periods of continued deep, dry coughing that are not due to other illnesses or to smoking

- periods of extreme and unexplainable fatigue that may be accompanied by headaches, lightheadedness and/or dizziness

- recurring fevers and/or night sweats

- rapid loss of more than 10 pounds of weight that is not due to increased physical exercise or dieting

- bruising more easily than normal

- unexplained bleeding from growths on the skin, from mucous membranes or from any opening in the body

- repeated occurrences of diarrhea

Whether or not such symptoms prove to be AIDS-related, a doctor should be consulted if any of these symptoms occur.

How is AIDS Diagnosed?

Diagnosis is based on several factors, including the state of a person's immune system, the presence of AIDS antibodies, and the presence of opportunistic infections and diseases associated with AIDS.

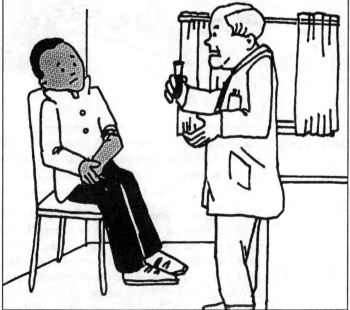

Diagnosis of AIDS is based on several factors.

How Can People Avoid Getting AIDS?

To avoid getting AIDS:

- When you have sex, follow "safer sex" guidelines:
  - know the partner's health status and whether or not he or she has other sex partners
  - do not exchange certain bodily fluids (blood and semen)
  - limit the number of sex partners (preferably to one person who has done the same)
  - use condoms
- never share needles to inject drugs (boiling does not guarantee sterility)
- do not share toothbrushes, razors, or other personal items that could be contaminated with blood
- maintain a strong immune system:
  - eat well
  - get enough rest and exercise
  - avoid recreational and illicit drugs
  - avoid heavy use of alcohol and tobacco
  - have regular medical checkups

People with AIDS, people who are at risk for AIDS and people who carry the AIDS virus must not donate blood, plasma, sperm, body organs, or other tissues.

Avoid risky behaviors.

How Do Women Get AIDS?

Like men, women can get AIDS by sharing needles with I.V. drug users or by having sexual intercourse involving exchange of bodily fluids with a person who has AIDS or who is infected with the AIDS virus. A few women have developed AIDS following transfusions of contaminated blood.

Any pregnant woman who knows or thinks she may carry the virus should immediately consult a health care provider who is knowledgeable about AIDS. It is also important to do so if her partner has AIDS if she or her partner is an I.V. drug user or if either is having other sexual relationships. Because the AIDS virus is very likely to spread from her to the fetus during pregnancy, and because AIDS is fatal to children born with the disease, a pregnant woman who tests positive for the AIDS virus may want to consider terminating her pregnancy.

Commonly Asked Questions About AIDS

Listed below are commonly asked questions about AIDS and the factual answers to these question:

Should mothers exposed to the AIDS virus breastfeed their infants?

No. Breastfeeding may spread AIDS from mother to child.

Is there a test to determine if a person has been exposed to AIDS?

Blood tests determining exposure to the AIDS virus are available through private physicians, hospital clinics and blood banks, as well as most local, state, and federal health departments. The tests are designed to detect antibodies to AIDS. The presence of AIDS antibodies in a person's blood means that he or she has been exposed to the AIDS virus, but does not mean that the person has, or will have AIDS. Though they are highly accurate, AIDS antibody tests can only be reliable in detecting infections that are more than four months old.

Who should be tested for antibodies to AIDS?

There are several considerations to make before deciding to be tested for antibodies to AIDS.

- Testing positive for AIDS antibodies does not mean that a person has, or will develop AIDS.

- Test results cannot distinguish persons who have developed an immunity to AIDS from those who have not.

- Positive test results, if leaked to an employer or insurance company, can lead to serious and prejudicial consequences.

- Since there is no medical treatment for a positive result, testing might lead to overwhelming anxiety and psychological distress.

- Birth control pills, alcoholism, and other factors may cause false positive results indicating infection when there is none.

Confidential testing may be appropriate, however, for people at risk for AIDS and/or for their partners who:

- are considering parenthood

- are considering enlistment in the armed forces

- have been exclusively monogamous for a number of years and wish to disregard safer sex guidelines

Is there a risk of getting AIDS from a blood transfusion?

Since May 1985, all blood donations are screened for antibodies to AIDS. Blood that tests positive for AIDS antibodies is not used for transfusions. Because the body takes a while to develop antibodies, however, there is a very small chance that a newly infected blood donor may not have developed AIDS antibodies between the time of exposure to the virus and the donation of blood. Nevertheless, the benefits of essential procedures outweigh the small risks of contracting AIDS through blood transfusion.

Is there a chance of getting AIDS by donating blood?

No. Blood banks and other blood collection centers use sterile, disposable needles and syringes that are used only once.

How is AIDS Treated?

Currently, there are no medicines that can cure AIDS and, for now, there is no vaccine to prevent it. Therapies are available to treat separately each of the many opportunistic diseases affecting people with AIDS, but these therapies vary in success from one person to another, and none of them is a permanent cure.

It is possible, though, to ease the burdens of this frightening, tragic and often lengthy illness. Many people with AIDS, their families, friends, neighbors, and health care workers have made major strides by coming to terms with the feelings of fear, helplessness, and inadequacy that surround AIDS. Learning to cope with the overwhelming personal catastrophe of AIDS has also led them to recognize that there are other non-medical elements that are essential in the treatment of people with AIDS.

People with AIDS not only require the most advance medicines and chemical therapies, they also require psychologically positive environments. The latest medical research indicates that there is a direct relationship between a person's psychological outlook and the function of his or her immune system. The ingredients for maintaining the healthy outlook of a person with AIDS are those of any normal and healthy life. They include:

- companionship
- access to a job
- access to social, educational, and recreational facilities
- access to places of worship in the community

Members of the community need to realize that no one has ever contracted AIDS in any way other than those listed previously.

- **IT IS NOT POSSIBLE TO GET AIDS** through casual contact with people who have it.
- **IT IS NOT POSSIBLE TO GET AIDS** by being around someone with it.
- **IT IS NOT POSSIBLE TO GET AIDS** by visiting, socializing, or working with someone who has it.
- **IT IS NOT POSSIBLE TO GET AIDS** by being sneezed upon, coughed upon, or breathed upon by anyone who has it.

Ignoring as Behavior Management

Ignoring is a form of behavior management used to reduce or eliminate behaivors of children parents find especially irritating. Ignoring is a way parents communicate their disapproval of certain behaviors by deliberately not paying attention in words or actions to undesirable behaviors whenever they occur. Not paying attention means absolutely no acknowledgement in any manner that the behavior is present.

Ignoring is not paying ANY attention to unwanted behaviors.

Ignoring is not threatening, hitting, or criticizing children because of some undesirable behavior. To criticize a behavior, parents have to pay attention to it. To some children, any kind of attention, even negative attention is reinforcing. By paying attention to the undesirable behavior, parents are actually encouraging children to continue to perform the behavior.

When to Ignore and When Not to Ignore

Parents may often wonder whether or not they should ignore certain behaviors. Certainly there are some behaviors that should be ignored and others that need the immediate attention of parents. Here are some helpful suggestions:

Degree of Potential Harm

Do not ignore any behavior that increases the risk of physical harm to the child or other children. Two examples of behaviors you should not ignore are playing with matches or inserting objects into an electrical outlet..

On the other hand, ignore behaviors such as whining and temper tantrums. It is unlikely that any of these behaviors will increase the risk of physical harm.

Damage To Property

Do not ignore behaviors that can damage or destroy property. Writing with spray paint on an interior or exterior wall, stepping on plants, or breaking toys are behaviors that require immediate action. You can effectively ignore other behaviors that have limited risk to the destruction of property.

Irritating Behaviors for Attention

Some behaviors that children perform are strictly for attention and most parents find these behaviors especially irritating. Nagging, quarreling, temper tantrums, whining, and interrupting are irritating behaviors. Children use these behaviors to get mom or dad to pay attention to them. Paying attention to these behaviors will only tend to reinforce their continued use. Remember, temper tantrums are not likely to happen if there is no one to watch them.

Do not ignore some behaviors you may find to be irritating. Crying because a child is frightened or hurt is not a behavior that will disappear if ignored. There is a greater chance that the behavior will stop if you hold and reassure the child. On the other hand, always ignore crying during a temper tantrum..

Before You Use Ignoring

1. Decide what behavior you want to see.

2. Be sure you can tolerate the behavior without eventually giving in or punishing the child.

3. Decide whether you can tolerate the behavior without having to remove the child from the area.

4. Be sure you can ignore the behavior 100% of the time no matter how long it lasts.

How to Ignore

1. **Ignoring means absolutely no attention.** Do not look at or talk to the child. Any attention, even threats and criticism, will reinforce the behavior. Focus your attention elsewhere. Dream your favorite day dream, plan your fantasy vacation, or relive a happy memory.

2. **The behavior may continue for one minute, 10 minutes, or 30 minutes. Ignore the entire time.** The behavior may turn for the worse before it gets better. If that happens, don't give in even though you may feel angry or embarrassed.

3. **When the behavior stops, praise the child immediately.** "I'm sure glad you stopped your temper tantrum. I don't like temper tantrums and it's much nicer to be with you when you aren't screaming." This is the good consequence. The child has now learned temper tantrums did not get your attention, but when he or she stopped, you gave your attention.

4. **If anyone else is reinforcing the inappropriate behavior, like a sympathetic grandparent, brother, or sister, you will have to convince them to ignore the behavior also.**

5. **When using ignoring as a technique in changing behavior, you do not ignore the child, you ignore the irritating behavior.** The child soon gets the message that even though you love him or her, you do not like the undesirable behavior.

Remember — praise the behavior you like, ignore the behavior you don't like.

Stimulating and Communicating

Talking to and touching your baby are two important things to do to help your child develop a good attitude about him or herself and about life in general. Let's examine why and how talking to and touching your child is important.

Children are born with the capacity to understand words and to learn to talk. In fact, children start to communicate their needs from the moment they are born. They just don't start using words until a couple of years later. When a baby hears his mother's voice, he will stop what he is doing and listen. When a child is almost four months old, when someone talks to him, he will respond with noises. The noises will not be words, but your baby is communicating.

Baby's First Sounds

The first sounds babies will make are sounds like **e's** and **eh's** and **a's**. Babies make these sounds when they need something. We call them "discomfort sounds." Another name for discomfort sounds is crying. Children will cry in sounds of **e, eh,** and **a**.

Soon babies learn other sounds like **ah, oh, oo**. We call them "comfort sounds" and you'll usually hear them when the baby feels content.

When you pay attention to the different sounds of comfort and discomfort, you are helping establish a way your baby can talk to you. The child learns that when he makes these noises, his mother will respond by doing something. These noises will begin to show up in combinations around six months of age. At this point, the baby will start to babble.

Reinforcing Baby's Sounds

Sometimes your baby will say something that sounds like a word, but isn't. Smile and praise your child for saying that noise. That's baby talk. Imitate that noise and say it back to him. When you imitate his sounds, he'll probably say them right back. Enjoy those sounds and give your child a hug. Tell him how pleased you are that he is talking.

Praise and imitate the noises your child makes.

Language Development

Talk to your children all the time. Talk when you're feeding them, changing their diapers, giving them a bath, or putting them to bed. Talk to them so they can learn to put words to certain actions and objects. We call this language development and it's very important for helping children express their needs in words. To help stimulate language development, read books with your children. Anytime during the day is a good time to read stories together, but it's an especially nice thing to do before children go to sleep.

Describing how children feel is another excellent time to help children develop their language. Use words to describe how you think your children are feeling: "Adam seems very sad right now," or "Tami is feeling happy." Putting words to feelings will help children express how they are feeling—a skill you certainly want to develop.

"Chad, you seem to be real happy."

Stimulating Your Child

You already are probably aware that young children are explorers in diapers. They love to touch and nothing is sacred. If it's in reach, the child will touch, grab, twist, bite, or pull on it. Of course you do want to baby proof your house to reduce the risk of injury to your child by putting unsafe objects and chemicals out of his reach. Give your child safe things to touch and play with.

Stimulating your child is very important to his overall development. We have listed several things you can do to help stimulate your child.

● Give your child safe things to touch of different textures: hard, soft, fuzzy, sticky, creamy, etc.

● Let your child play with objects of different colors and sizes.

● Have colored shapes, pictures of animals, and books nearby the changing table. When your child gets bored with having his diaper changed, he can look at pictures instead.

● Hang mobiles by the changing table or above his bed. Make sure they are the kind your baby can see when he is laying down looking up. Also, make sure the mobiles are not accessible for your baby to pull himself up, or get tangled up in.

● Dance with and sing to your baby. Babies love gentle rhythmic movements.

● Stimulate your child's awareness of his body by giving him a massage. You know how nice massages feel.

These are some simple suggestions for talking and stimulating your child. A conscious effort on your part will encourage your child to find life exciting and wonderful.

Establishing Nurturing Routines

A routine is a consistent way of doing things. Routines are usually established by parents to manage their own behavior and the behavior of their children. Some family routines may be cleaning the home on Saturday mornings, doing laundry on Wednesday evenings, saying grace at the dinner table, etc.

A family routine could be cleaning on Saturday mornings.

A nurturing routine is a consistent way of doing things that promotes a child's self-concept and self-esteem. Nurturing routines are established by parents to reinforce the positive overall growth of their children. Nurturing routines tell kids that the way to do things in our family helps everyone feel good about themselves. Feeling good about yourself is very important for acting appropriately and doing good things.

Nurturing routines help establish consistency. Children feel secure when they know what to expect. The security they feel allows them to learn to trust people important to them, like their mother and father. From trusting parents comes the natural response of being able to trust others.

Nurturing routines help establish a positive self-esteem and positive self-concept in children. Positive thoughts and feelings toward oneself are two important personality traits which emerge from nurturing routines. Without positive feelings and thoughts about oneself, there is little chance that the child will treat others with respect and kindness. Since he feels and thinks badly about himself, it's likely that he will feel and think badly about others. Nurturing routines help children develop a positive regard for themselves which leads to a positive regard for others.

Nurturing routines help establish empathy. Doing something consistently, and doing it with concern for a child's self-concept and self-esteem, helps the child develop a sense of trust. Children learn that adults are people who care for them and help them get their needs met. This feeling of trust leads to feelings of caring for others as the child continues to mature. Empathy, the awareness of the needs of others, is a primary and necessary characteristic of nurturing parents and children.

Important Ingredients in Nurturing Routines

Nurturing routines consist of:

- Gentle, positive touch: hugs, kisses, tickles, massages

- Praise for being and doing: "Mommy really loves you" (being); "What a good listener you are" (doing)

- Happy, pleasant expressions and tone of voice: smiles; light cheerful voice

- Caring, empathic caregivers: being aware of the needs of children

- Fun: games, finger plays, songs, dance

- Consistency: being predictable

Types of Nurturing Routines

Establish nurturing routines in the following areas of parent-child interactions:

- Diapering and Dressing Time

- Feeding Time

- Bath Time

- Bedtime

When is it Best to Begin Nurturing Routines?

Parents should begin to establish nurturing routines the moment they bring their baby home. Starting early is the best way to establish consistent, caring and loving parent-child interactions.

The Nurturing Program helps parents learn to establish nurturing routines with their children, ages birth to five years.

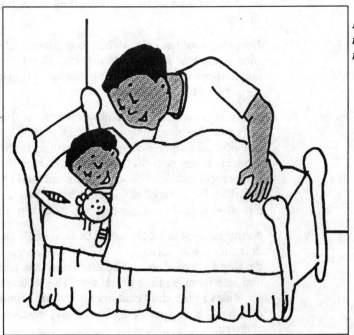

Practice nurturing routines daily.

Nurturing Diapering and Dressing Routines

Diapering and dressing children are excellent times to use nurturing routines. During these times, parents can encourage enormous growth in the child's sense of independence and cooperation, as well as in positive nurturing touch. Let's take a closer look at how parents can establish a nurturing diapering and dressing routine.

Learning Independence While Dressing

Children like to do things for themselves as quickly as they can. You can see it very early when infants repeatedly try to stand and walk only to fall flat on their bottoms. You can also see it when they attempt to feed themselves by smearing food all over their faces with the hope that some of it will get in their mouths. Little successes in these and other tasks result in great joy because children are finally learning to do things for themselves. These accomplishments have greater value in that they help establish in children a sense of independence and cooperation. When children learn independence and cooperation, they learn to do more things for themselves and by themselves. To help your children learn to be independent and cooperative, parents need to learn the major rule in dressing children: diapering and dressing children is a partnership between the parent and the child.

As a partnership, you and your child work together as a team in getting clothes on and off your child. The following steps are suggested to make dressing your child a pleasant experience.

1. Let your child have input into what she is to wear for the day. You might do this by selecting two tops and two bottoms. Have your child make the choice which top and bottom she wants to wear. In this way, your child is taking an active role in getting dressed. Also in a partnership, your child is taking an active role in getting dressed and undressed rather than the passive role most children experience. Too many parents dress or undress their child without the child's active assistance. The active partnership role builds independence and cooperation.

2. Allow your child to do the things she can do by herself without any help from you. If she can put her socks on, fine, let her do it by herself. If it's pulling up her pants, good, don't do it for her. Let her pull her own pants up.

3. Assist your child in getting dressed but allow her to still have the lead. In this step, you're only assisting your child in doing things she can't quite do alone yet — like, putting pants on, or putting a tee shirt on.

4. Take the lead in assisting your child in getting dressed. In the last step, you do the things your child is incapable of doing. It might be putting on and tying shoes, zipping zippers, buttoning buttons, etc. In step four, the child hasn't yet developed the skills needed to finish getting dressed. As your child develops more skills, the need for step four is less and less.

Diapering and dressing children is a partnership between the parent and child.

Knowing When to Use the Steps

To assist you in knowing what steps to use and when to use them, here are some suggestions.

1. Observe your child and make it a point of knowing what your child is capable of doing independently. The younger the child, the more quickly these skills will change on a daily and weekly basis.

2. When you are quite sure of the things your child can do by herself, break the things she can't do into smaller steps. The smaller steps will allow her to continue to gain further feelings of confidence. Let's take the activity of putting on a pair of pants. First, have her sit in a chair without you placing her there if she can do it by herself. Second, gather the pant legs and make doughnuts. Lay them on the floor just in front of her feet. Third, tell her to step into the holes and ease the pants around her ankles. Fourth, have her take hold of one or both sides and "pull up." If she is very young, she probably doesn't have strength to pull the pants up all the way so you will have to help. Fifth, you do the snapping of the pants if it's something she can't do by herself.

Partnership Method Begins at Birth

Babies participate in the partnership method of getting dressed and many parents aren't even aware of it. When babies are getting their diapers changed, they participate in the partnership method by laying still while mom or dad is putting a clean diaper on. Although this level of partnership may seem slight, for the developmental level of the children it is indeed very active.

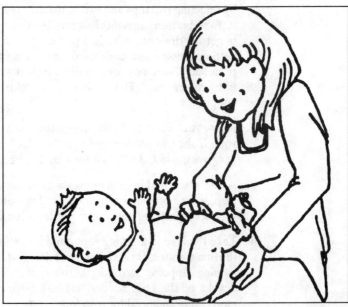

Infants also participate in partnership while diapering.

Young infants also are active participants in getting themselves dressed by holding their arms and legs up. They help by putting their arms through the sleeve openings. If you watch closely, you'll notice all the things your young infant can do with a little assistance.

There you have it, the partnership method of helping your children get dressed. It takes a lot more time than getting your child dressed while he or she stands passively waiting for you to finish. However, the time you spend in establishing a nurturing dressing routine when your child is young will pay off later when your child is capable, cooperative, and independent.

Nurturing Feeding Time Routines

Eating is one of the most pleasurable times during infancy and young childhood. Babies love to eat. In fact, most babies double their birth weight in the first three to five months of life. That's a lot of eating! If they could talk, babies would probably tell us that nothing in this world is as good as sucking on a nipple and getting milk or juice. Watch them when they are sucking: they relax, begin to coo, close their eyes and fall asleep. Parents are probably pleased when babies eat because the child quiets down and is more pleasant to be with.

Babies find great relaxation and joy in sucking.

As children grow older, something happens that changes all this pure pleasure into frustration, dissatisfaction, and stress for both the children and the parents. Children refuse to eat certain foods, are attracted to "junk" foods, and snack between meals. They begin to hate the very foods the parents feel are best for them. What happens?

The Importance of Feeding Times

To begin to understand how feeding and eating begin to go sour, let's first discuss some common facts about children's eating habits.

- Despite some popular beliefs, babies know how many calories they need and what their stomachs can handle. If babies are not getting enough, they'll want more. If they get too much, they will stop sucking.

- Feeding is one of the earliest experiences babies have. As such, they begin to learn a lot about themselves and the world they live in. Good experiences in feeding lead to good feelings of self and the world. Bad experiences lead to bad feelings toward themselves and their world.

- Babies will normally lose weight immediately after birth, but gradually begin to gain back lost weight in two or three days. Expect this weight loss.

- Somewhere around a year old, babies begin to change their feelings about food. They become more choosy and less hungry. What might look good to eat today won't look good tomorrow. Their choice of certain foods is the beginning of exerting autonomy and control of their lives.

- Teething often takes away children's appetites, especially when the first molars are beginning to come in.

- As children become more mobile (around one year), they may lose interest in eating. They often feel too busy exploring the environment and practicing new motor skills to sit still and eat.

Establishing a Nurturing Feeding Time Routine

The following steps are suggested to make feeding your child a more pleasant experience.

1. **Provide your child with a comfortable eating environment.** Put young babies in infant seats securely stationed on a table. Put older children in highchairs that stand on the floor. The comfortable eating environment provides the child with feelings of security. Padded cushions and straps to keep your child snug in the seat are essential.

2. **Allow your child the opportunity to reject food.** When you honor the request, you are reinforcing feelings of personal power. Remember, children know when they are not hungry. They also know when they don't like something just like you and I do. When you force your child to take "one more bite" of foods he doesn't like, you're actually setting up a conflict situation. In this situation, the child will end up the loser.

3. **Reinforce personal choice in eating.** Get in the habit of giving small portions. If the child wants more, he'll let you know. Making children sit at the table until they clean their plates does not build healthy attitudes toward eating.

4. **Try to get children to think of food as something they want, not something they need to reject.** One way to encourage positive attitudes toward food is to allow your child to eat larger than usual amounts of one wholesome food than others. Remember, the older the child gets, the more his attitudes and tastes are changing. Continue to offer servings of your child's less preferred food.

5. **Encourage your child to begin to feed himself around nine to ten months.** Practice with finger foods, bread crusts, and other foods. Children will want to pick up the food with their fingers. Let them. Expect a lot of accidental messes. If you're worried about the rug, put some plastic under the highchair.

6. **Encourage your child to use a spoon.** Give him reason to use it. At the beginning of the meal when he's the hungriest, let him try to get food on the spoon and into his mouth. Assist your child in feeding himself with a spoon. Praise his efforts; tell him how proud you are he is trying to feed himself.

7. **Don't worry about table manners.** Touching, smashing, squeezing, and smearing food is an early form of child's play. Don't punish your child or take his food away. Remember, building positive attitudes toward food and eating is nearly as important as the actual eating of the food.

8. **Praise your child.** There are many behaviors you can praise. Some are feeding himself, eating a wholesome meal, sitting patiently waiting for food, using a fork or spoon, or wiping his face. Remember, praise the behavior you want.

"You are doing a nice job of feeding yourself."

Nutritious Foods for Children

Vegetable and Fruit Group

Apples, peaches, pears, grapes, etc.

Raw vegetable sticks or pieces (radishes, celery, cauliflower, green onions, zucchini, green peppers, carrots, cucumbers — even parsnips!)

Dried apricots, raisins, prunes

Canned fruits or fruit juices kept chilled in the refrigerator

Ripe tomatoes — eat 'em right out of your hand!

Mini-kabobs of bite-sized fruit chunks, strung on a toothpick

Banana chunks dipped in orange juice. Shake in a bag with chopped peanuts. Spear with toothpicks

Celery stuffed with cottage cheese, cheese spread, or peanut butter

Juice cubes you make by freezing fruit juice in an ice cube tray. Chill other fruit drinks with them

Chilled cranberry juice mixed with club soda

Grapefruit half, sprinkled with brown sugar and broiled

Tomato half, sprinkled with breadcrumbs, parmesan or grated cheddar cheese and broiled

Creative salads of lettuce, raw spinach and other fresh vegetables, fruits, meats, eggs, or seafood

Quick and easy vegetables and fruit.

Nutritious Foods for Children

Bread and Cereal Group

Raisin bread, toasted and spread with peanut butter

Sandwiches using a variety of breads—raisin, cracked wheat, pumpernickel, rye, black

Date-nut roll or brown bread spread with cream cheese

English muffins, served open-faced for sandwiches such as hot roast beef or turkey, chicken salad, sloppy joes

Individual pizzas. Top english muffin halves with cheese slices, tomato sauce and oregano, and broil

Waffles topped with whipped topping and strawberries

Wheat or rye crackers topped with herb-seasoned cottage cheese, cheese or meat spread, or peanut butter

Graham crackers and milk

Ready-to-eat cereals right out of the box!

Ice cream or pudding, sprinkled with crisp cereals or wheat germ

Quick and easy bread and cereal recipes.

Nutritious Foods for Children

Meat, Poultry, Fish, and Beans Group

Nuts, sesame seeds, or toasted sunflower seeds

Sandwich spread of peanut butter combined with raisins or chopped dates

Peanut butter and honey spread on an English muffin, sprinkled with chopped walnuts, and heated under broiler

Grilled open-faced peanut butter and mashed banana sandwich

Tomatoes stuffed with egg salad

Melon wedges topped with thinly sliced ham

Sandwich of cheese, meat, tomato, onion, and lettuce

Antipasto of tuna, shrimp, anchovies, hardcooked eggs and assorted vegetables

Leftover poultry or meat—as is, or chopped into a sandwich spread

Bite-sized cubes of broiled beef, served on a toothpick

Quick and easy recipes to enjoy.

Nutritious Foods for Children

Milk and Cheese Group

Milk shakes with mashed fresh berries or bananas

Parfait of cottage cheese, yogurt, or ice milk combined with fruit, sprinkled with chopped nuts, wheat germ, or crisp cereal

Dips for vegetable sticks. For fewer calories, substitute cottage cheese or plain yogurt for sour cream and mayonnaise in preparing dips

Fruit-flavored yogurt

Cheese cubes, au naturel, or speared with pretzel sticks, or alternated with mandarin orange sections on a toothpick

Custard or pudding

Ice milk sundae, topped with fresh canned, or frozen fruits

Quick and easy dairy snacks.

Taken From: Food, Home and Garden Bulletin Number 228; prepared by Science and Education Adm., U.S. Department of Agriculture

Tips For Cooking With Children

1. Do your food prejudices show? **You** are the model; don't let your likes and dislikes influence the selection of food experiences.

2. Objective: To encourage the consumption of a variety of wholesome foods through positive experiences with foods.

3. Stress food in its natural state. Allow children to see, smell, feel, and taste the food at different stages of preparation. Compare colors and textures, shapes and sizes.

4. Choose simple cooking experiences first. As children master basic manipulative skill, gradually add more learning steps.

5. Develop "picture recipes" including utensils and illustrated measurement of ingredients.

6. Review the picture recipe and all directions before beginning a food activity.

7. Have all utensils ready ahead of time.

8. Sanitation: Does everyone have clean hands? Wash hands and work surface before starting. Explain what to do if child has to sneeze or cough.

9. Safety: Teach for awareness of sharp objects and hot surfaces. Children use knives and graters only under close supervision.

10. Supervision: Recommendation of one adult to every five to six children.

11. Planning: Coordinate cooking (food activities) with the class day. Build a food experience into multi-learning experiences— math, art, science, language, social science, safety, courtesy, **and nutrition.**

Choose simple recipes and keep your group small.

Nutrition Education and Training Program, Food and Nutrition Services Section, Wisconsin Department of Public Instruction

Families And Chemical Use Questionnaire

The following questions are designed to only increase your awareness about your chemical use and the chemical use of any family member. The word "chemical" in these questions refers to all mood altering substances such as alcohol, pot, speed, uppers, downers, etc. Answer the questions as honestly as you can. You will not be required to turn this questionnaire in to anyone.

About You	Yes	No
1. Do you feel you have a chemical use (pot, alcohol, speed, downers, uppers, etc.) problem?		
2. Do you often use a chemical to feel better?		
3. Do you often use a chemical to "get through the day?"		
4. Do you spend more money on your chemical than you planned?		
5. Do you feel annoyed or irritated if your family or friends discuss your chemical use?		
6. Have you had any arguments with your family or friends because of your chemical use?		
7. Have you ever failed to keep a promise you made to yourself about cutting down on your chemical use?		
8. Do you tend to use your chemical at times when you feel angry, disappointed, depressed, anxious, or lonely?		
9. Have you ever been careless of your family's welfare when you've been using a chemical? (Driving under the influence, falling asleep with a burning cigarette, not caring where your kids were, blowing a paycheck on chemicals, hitting a family member when under the influence?)		
10. Do you use chemicals in the morning to help you recover from the night before?		

About Your Family		
1. Do you feel a member of your family has a chemical use problem?		
2. Do you lie awake worrying about your family member (of whatever age)?		
3. Do you feel frustrated in your attempts to control your family member?		
4. Do you argue with your family member about his or her use of chemicals?		
5. Do you find it increasingly difficult to communicate with your family member?		
6. Do you find yourself lying or covering up for your family member?		
7. Do you feel resentful or hostile toward your family member?		
8. Do you worry about your family member's behavior affecting other members of the family?		
9. Has the family member been confronted about his/her use of chemicals?		
10. Has the family member denied his/her use of chemicals?		

Nurturing Bath Time Routine

For many young children, getting into a bathtub of warm water is not one of their favorite things to do. However, almost all children love to walk in standing puddles, splash water on others, and run through open sprinklers. So why is bath time a time of frustration, tears, and stress for children and their parents? Let's examine why.

There are several reasons why your son or daughter may experience bath time as a bad time.

- **Most bath times come at the end of the day.** Not only may young children be overtired, but parents may be feeling the stress of their day. They communicate this stress by being a bit more demanding that their children cooperate. Children easily pick up on the parent's anxiety and become anxious themselves.

- **Because taking a bath comes at the end of the day, bath time is usually followed by bedtime.** Children soon learn that taking a bath means soon they will have to go to bed. If a child wishes to stay up longer, the obvious reaction is to resist taking a bath.

- **Many parents treat bath time as a chore rather than a time for fun, relaxation, and enjoyment.** An attitude of "having to take a bath" is established rather than an attitude of "wanting to take a bath."

- **Bath time for children in some families is often an "on again-off again" occurrence.** Sometimes children have to take baths, sometimes they don't. Although parents may have good rationale for excluding a child's bath, children, especially young children, don't understand why on some days they have to take a bath and on other days they don't. What they experience is inconsistency. This leads to feelings of anxiety exhibited as resistance.

- **The experience of taking a bath may be a very unpleasant and frightening one for many children.** Soap in eyes, hot water burns, accidental falls, pouring water on a child's head to rinse shampoo, etc. are all things that can make bath time a bad time.

Bath time can be frightening to some children.

How to Make Bath Time a Fun Time

For children to want to take a bath more often than not, bath time has to be a fun time. The following suggestions are recommended for developing a positive, nurturing routine for giving children baths.

1. **Make bath time sound like a fun time**. Young children like to pretend. Give the bathtub a name or refer to it as "tubby time" with a sound of happiness. Pretend the tubby can talk and call the child's name, "Chris, I'm waiting for you." You can then answer back, "We're coming tubby." It's quite a bit better than saying, "Chris, I want you to take your bath now!"

2. **Let your child turn the water on and fill the tub**. Giving the child more responsibility in keeping himself clean is the ultimate goal. Allow him to put the bubble bath in, set the water temperature, and fill the tub to the desired depth.

3. **Encourage your child to play in the tub.** Bring in "tubby toys" for the child to play with; they don't have to be anything fancy. Use plastic cups, bowls, empty plastic dish detergent containers or plastic syrup containers with the plastic pour spouts, etc. Anything that floats, squirts water, holds or pours water will work.

4. **Encourage your child to get to know his/her body.** Tubby time is a great time for body exploration and recognition of body parts. Give your child's body parts names and use the names when washing your child: "Look, I see Adam's hands. Oh, boy! Adam's hands need a washing!"

5. **Take a bath with your child(ren).** Children think it's fun taking a bath with their mom or dad. Singing, playing with toys, and washing all help the child feel more comfortable when mom or dad are also in the tub.

6. **Make the experience of tubby time enjoyable.** Several things you can do to help make the experience of taking a bath more enjoyable:

   - Use mild soaps and shampoos to avoid eye sting.

   - Place a mat on the bottom of the tub to prevent accidental slipping.

   - Protect against accidents by placing foam rubber guards over the water spout.

   - Get each of your children their own towel to dry themselves and their own robe to wear after taking a bath.

7. **Make tubby time a daily routine.** If children know every day they will have a tubby time, soon they will come to accept it as a daily routine. Consistency will help lessen the uncertainty and reduce the anxiety of not knowing.

Words of Caution

Never, ever, leave a very young child alone in the bathtub. Accidental drowning and other injuries can occur in a matter of seconds and minutes.

Keep all electrical appliances unplugged and away from the grasp of children. Water and electricity are deadly together. For the sake of your family's welfare, keep all electrical appliances safely stored in a locked cabinet or closet.

Make bath time a safe, fun time for your children.

Nurturing Bedtime Routine

At some point in almost every child's life, getting ready for bed and going to sleep are two of the least favorite things to do. Much to the heartache of many parents, trying to get children to take naps and get plenty of sleep often results in a lot of stress and frustration for the children and parents. Not surprisingly, in some families, bedtime becomes a battle time. In these families, both the parents and children end up losing.

Many experts believe that bedtime is one of the most important times for children to learn positive feelings about themselves and others in their world, particularly mom and dad. Unfortunately, becauce a lot of arguing and tension exists between parents and children during bedtime, what is learned and established is not positive at all. Establishing a nurturing routine at bedtime, one in which parents and children feel good about themselves and toward each other, is very important. Before we discuss how to establish a nurturing bedtime routine, let's examine why bedtime problems occur.

Bedtime Problems

Probably the single biggest contributing factor for young children to dislike going to bed is the anxiety they feel in being separated from their mothers. Remember, moms are very important to children for their survival. When they are not in view of the infant, feelings of fear set in. The term used to describe this fear is "separation anxiety." Separation anxiety results when children fear being left alone or unattended. Excessive crying and temper tantrums are two common behaviors associated with separation anxiety. Letting children know you haven't abandoned them at nighttime is very important in helping them build feelings of trust and security. Reassuring the child with kind words and a gentle touch helps reduce anxiety. As children get older, their fears of separation generally lessen and nighttime becomes a more peaceful time.

Infants face another type of nighttime problem, one a little bit easier to solve. The problem is hunger. Infants get hungry during the night and need to be fed. Usually when fed, the baby will fall back asleep only to awaken when he's hungry again.

Many children three years and older have difficulty going to sleep at night because of nighttime fears. Wetting, for children who are potty trained, may be a sign of nighttime fears. Ghosts, boogeymen, monsters, and demons are all very real for some children who feel vulnerable at night. Nightmares may result, which only tend to reinforce a child's fear of the dark. In this sense, children don't want to go to sleep because they are afraid and insecure. Talking about their fears and getting older generally help children overcome them.

Another reason why some children may be reluctant to go to bed has more to do with what else is going on in the house. If nighttime is a time when the entire family plays games together, favorite guests come over, or favorite television programs are on, children may not want to go to bed. They feel excluded and would rather be up having fun. To avoid this situation, make sure all family play time occurs before bedtime for the youngest child.

Lastly, many children have a difficult time sleeping in their own room at night because of the time spent there as a punishment during the day. Being "sent to your room," where some children have to stay for hours, does not encourage children to associate their room with happy, pleasant feelings. Rather, children think of their rooms as a prison. If you're using time-out as punishment, use the living room or kitchen, not the child's bedroom.

Building a Nurturing Bedtime Routine

To make bedtime a more pleasant experience, the following ten steps are suggested.

1. **Identify a consistent time your child will be going to bed.** Inconsistent bedtime only creates confusion which leads to resentment. Identify a bedtime and stick to it.

2. **Make a nice relaxing bath time part of the nighttime routine for going to bed.** A nurturing bath time routine will serve as a positive preview for what's to come in getting ready for bed.

3. **Dress your child in clothes (pajamas, sleepers, etc.) especially for bedtime.** Getting dressed in these clothes is an indication that it's getting close to bedtime. If you can, get fun bedtime clothes with pictures of animals, cars, or cartoon characters on them. Getting dressed for bed will be even more fun.

4. **Help the child get dressed for sleep in his bedroom, not in other rooms of the house.** Keep the association between bed, sleep, and bedtime clothes intact.

5. **Have your child brush his/her teeth every night as part of the bedtime routine.** What an excellent habit to develop at a young age. Model the way to brush teeth by brushing your own. Giving your child his/her own toothbrush to play with and use is strongly recommended as part of the bedtime routine.

6. **Spend time with your child reading stories.** Find a cozy rocking chair and have your child crawl up on your lap. Get snuggled in, and read for awhile.

7. **Choose bedtime books that are happy and pleasing — books which add comfort not discomfort.** Save the scary stories for daytime reading when the child gets older. By the way, you might want to negotiate with your child how many stories you are going to read.

8. **When finished reading, tell your child it's time to lay down in the bed.** We recommend putting your child in the bed before he is asleep. Some children who fall asleep in their parent's arms wake up during the night and wonder where mommy and daddy went. Putting him down before he is asleep serves to get the child used to falling asleep alone. Then nighttime awakenings aren't as scary.

9. **Tuck your child in, make sure you tell him at least one nice thing he did, or how much you love him as a person, give him a hug or kiss, and wish him good dreams.** If you can, sing a song or two, help him relax and get cozy.

10. **If your child should begin to cry during the night, go into his room, and find out what the problem is.** Remember, crying is a signal of distress. The child is asking for help. Find out what he needs. Maybe a bottle, a blanket, a little reassuring is all that is needed for him to fall back to sleep.

Make bedtime a happy, pleasant experience.

Bedtime Myths

There are a couple of myths about bedtime parenting practices passed on from one generation of parents to another without any real evidence of their harmful effects. These myths confuse parents and limit their ability to be nurturing parents. Let's examine these bedtime myths and present the facts.

Myth:

Paying attention to a crying baby at night will only tend to reinforce the crying.

Fact:

It will if the **only** time you pay attention to your child is when he is crying. Remember what you pay attention to is what you get more of. If you pay a lot of attention to your child when he is not crying, his need to cry to get attention is lessened. Contrary to popular belief, a child whose needs are met and who receives a lot of attention will stand a better chance of feeling secure and trusting.

Myth:

Never let your child sleep in your bed; you'll never be able to get him out.

Fact:

Children like to feel close to their mom and dad. Feeling close is necessary in building trust and security. Occasionally crawling in bed with mom and dad because of illness, feeling scared, or just wanting to be close is okay. We do not encourage a daily habit of sleeping with mom and dad for several practical reasons: mom and dad need private time alone; reading or talking in bed might wake the child; the size of the bed may not be conducive for three or more family members; and, allowing a child to have his or her own private space is healthy for the child.

It is OK to ocasionally sleep with mom and dad in their bed.

Like all the other routines discussed in the Nurturing Program, establishing the bed time nurturing routine presented here takes more time and directed energy than a more inconsistent approach. You will realize the positive benefits of establishing nurturing routines in happier, healthier family interactions.

Toilet Training

Toilet training is not as hard as perhaps you are imagining. With careful planning and the right conditions, children can learn to use a potty chair in a matter of a few days to a few weeks. Before you begin toilet training, there are many important things that must be checked first.

Is Your Child Ready?

Age

Don't bother to begin teaching your child how to use the toilet if he is not at least two years old. Many children are trained when they are around two years old. If you plan on starting before two years of age, you will create undo anxiety in you and your child. This anxiety is likely to lead your child to feelings of failure, and a low self-concept.

Muscle Control

Can your child walk yet? Can he put little objects into bigger objects? Does he have good muscle control? If he doesn't, he won't be able to control his bladder or bowels. Physical coordination is necessary before you begin toilet training.

Physical Development

The maturity of the bladder is also important to consider. A couple of indicators that suggest your child's bladder capacity is ready for toilet training: a dry diaper after napping, and a steady flow of urine rather than several episodes of dribbles.

Communication

Your child will have to be able to communicate his intentions to urinate or have a bowel movement before you start successful toilet training. He has to be able to make some sound, make some facial expression, or physical movement to let you know he has to go. If he cannot communicate his intentions, he's not ready to learn to use the potty.

Follow Verbal Instructions

Your child will have to be able to follow instructions before you can start successful toilet training. Give your child verbal instructions like "hurry and go use the potty." See if he can follow through. If he can't, successful toilet training will not be accomplished.

Desire

Lastly, you have to determine whether or not your child has the desire to learn. All the other preconditions listed will serve little value if your child simply refuses to use the potty. Desire to use the potty will speed up the learning process.

Make sure your child is ready with the appropriate skills before you begin toilet training.

Before You Begin

The following suggestions will help you prepare your child to use the potty chair.

1. **Pick out appropriate words your child can use.** Parents need to help children decide on words to say when they need to urinate or have a bowel movement. Use any words you like, but it helps if the words make sense. If the words make sense, others can understand your child's needs when you're not around. Some words parents use are silly, confusing, and eventually embarrassing. Words like tinkle, shimkle, udo, shooo-shooo, wee wee, tee tee, #1 or #2, kaka, or BM all mean the child has to urinate or have a bowel movement. The words the child will use depends a great deal on the preference of the parents. Keep the words simple so a child can say them, yet understandable enough for others.

2. **Model the appropriate behavior.** Let the child see you and other family members using the toilet. When you urinate, you can say "Mommy (Daddy) is going pee pee in the toilet." That way your daughter or son notices how adults use the toilet. The same sex parent as child is preferable. Children may become confused watching family members of the opposite sex urinate. If you're a bit embarrassed by the thought of your child watching you use the toilet, ask an older son or daughter. Older siblings generally don't mind using the toilet with their younger brother or sister around.

3. **Buy a potty chair.** Before you begin toilet training, buy a potty chair. Purchasing a potty chair encourages your child to see, play, and become familiar with it before he begins to use it.

   We consider the separate unit potty chair, one that stands on the floor, better than the unit that attaches to the toilet. The separate standing unit allows the child to place his feet on the floor which adds to feelings of security and comfort.

   Let the child examine the potty, play with it, take it apart, and carry it around. Again, the more comfortable the child is with the potty, the greater the chance that he will want to use it.

Let your child play with the potty chair and get used to it.

4. **Buy training pants.** Your child will need to wear training pants instead of diapers when you begin toilet training. Help him learn to pull them up and pull them down. Fancy looking training pants with pictures of your child's favorite TV or cartoon character might make it a bit more enjoyable to wear training pants. If your child is still in diapers, do not attempt to start toilet training. There will be just too much frustration in getting the diaper off in time to use the potty.

5. **When you decide your child is ready to learn how to use the potty chair, try to pick a good day to begin.** It will help both you and your child to begin toilet training if both of you are in good moods. A cranky child, or one who has had a bad night's sleep, can make the task of toilet training very frustrating. In this situation, the parents who desire to teach the child may also become frustrated and unknowingly non-supportive and even punitive. Teaching your child to use the potty should be fun, not confrontive. Plan to set aside the entire day for helping and supporting your child. Make the task of introducing the potty your only task for the day.

Steps to Follow

1. **Try to make a realistic guess when your child will likely need to use the potty.** Is it after lunch, before nap, after nap, or after breakfast? Being aware of those times helps you to be available to possible potty times.

2. **When you notice your child is about to urinate or have a bowel movement, help him pull his pants down, and guide him to the potty.**

3. **Talk to your child.** Use the words you decided on for urination and bowel movement. Say to your child, "Adam is about ready to make poo poo in his potty. Oh, what an exciting time."

4. **Stay with your child in the bathroom while he is having a bowel movement.** Keep him company, read a story or two.

5. **Praise his efforts.** It might take some children a while to do their bowel movement. Don't pressure your child, support him.

6. **When he is finished, praise your child.** Don't be afraid to let him know how proud you are of his efforts, not of him. Children are anxious to get their parents' attention and approval. Don't be stingy with your praise.

7. **Teach your child how to wipe himself.** Teach girls to always wipe themselves from front to back. It's a good habit to start early, one that will help prevent bladder infections in the future.

8. **After your child has gone in the potty, you can empty the potty in several ways:**

   - You can empty the potty in the toilet and flush the toilet while your child watches.

   - Your child can help you empty the potty by flushing the toilet.

   - You can empty the potty after your child has left the room.

Some children are very sensitive and may become upset that a product of their body is disappearing. You may not want to flush the toilet until they leave the room. Other children worry less about that issue and may want to take an active role in discarding the potty material. Be sensitive to your child's needs and act accordingly.

Accidents Will Happen

Expect that your child will have accidents in the beginning. Accidents are a normal occurrence. When an accident happens, talk to your child and reassure him. "Oh Oh. Adam made poo poo in his pants. Too bad. Next time Adam will do poo poo in the potty. Let's change your pants. Poo poo in your pants probably doesn't feel very good." The main thing to remember when accidents happen: **Do not make a big deal about them.** Make a big deal when your child uses the potty.

Expect accidents in the beginning and give reassurance.

If your child misses the potty and wets or soils the floor, reassuringly tell him, "Oh Adam missed the potty this time. Can you put your pee pee or poo poo in the potty next time? Thanks for trying son!" Always encourage your child to use the potty.

If your child begins to act as if he never heard of, let alone used a potty, remain supportive and talk to your child. Several things may be going on that could be contributing to your child's regressing:

- The child feels less attention is being paid to him.

- A new brother or sister in the family has taken over the spotlight.

- Too much pressure is being put on using the potty correctly.

- Family problems, separations, divorces, extended absences, moving to a new home, illness, etc.

If your child continues to wet and soil himself, put him back in diapers. This way the pressure is lessened for you and for him.

Some Final Points to Remember

- Never, ever use punishment in teaching your child to use the potty. Punitive, abusive practices only cause increased anxiety and can lead to very severe problems. We cannot stress enough that punishment is harmful in teaching children to use the potty.

- Once your child has begun to use the potty, keep the potty in the bathroom. Don't get into the habit of moving the potty in front of the TV to amuse your child. You don't move your toilet in front of the TV, so don't move the potty. The bathroom is the place where toilets and potties belong.

Keep your child's potty in the bathroom.

- Children are constantly learning who they are and what values they have from the important people in their lives. Parents are probably the most important of all the people children interact with. Teaching your child to use the toilet is an important time between both of you. Through your teaching and support, help your child realize that he or she is a winner: someone you are proud of, someone you enjoy being with, someone who tries real hard.

The greatest single outcome a child can learn from the whole experience of toilet training is positive regard for himself. Keep this fact in mind as you're helping your child learn to use the potty.

Home-Based Home Practice Exercises

Following are Home Practice Exercises for you to complete. They will help you practice the new skills you learned during each session. Write your response on a separate sheet of paper. Do your best and share your responses with your home visitor during the next session.

Session 1

Before next session:

- Read the information entitled **Program Orientation**, pages 1-2 in your Handbook.

- Spend 30 minutes each day with each of your children in nurturing play time activities. Play time is a time with you and your children alone — no TV, no other distractions. Playing a game and reading books are good activities. Practice the activities listed in the *Activities Manual for Infants*, *Activities Manual for Toddlers*, or *Activities Manual for Preschoolers*. Add information to the *Memories and Developmental Milestones* booklet. Remember what you did and report next week.

If grandparents are participating, complete the following additional tasks.

Family Home Nurturing Hour

- Identify the specific role of the teen parent in raising the child.

- Identify the specific role of the grandparents in raising the child.

- Identify the issues that need to be worked out between the grandparents and teen parents. Make a list and be very clear in what needs to be worked on. Bring the list to the next session.

- End the hour with a family hug.

Session 2

Before next session:

- Read the information entitled **Nurturing Program for Teenage Parents and Their Families**, pages 3-5 in your Handbook.

- Spend 30 minutes each day with each of your children in nurturing play time activities. Play time is a time you and your children do fun things together. Use the activities presented in the nurturing booklets: *Activities Manual for Infants*, *Activities Manual for Toddlers*, or *Activities Manual for Preschoolers*. Add information to the *Memories and Developmental Milestones* booklet. Remember what you did and report next week.

(continued on next page)

Session 2 (continued)

If grandparents are participating, complete the following additional tasks.

Family Home Nurturing Hour

- Teen parents and grandparents take turns responding to the following statements:

  ° The one thing I want to learn most of all from this program is _____ .

  ° For my child/grandchild to grow up healthy, what he/she needs most from me is _____ .

  ° The one parenting quality that we need most to work on is _____ .

- End the hour with a family hug.

Session 3

Before next session:

- Spend 30 minutes of play time with each of your children each day. Play time is a time you and your children do fun things together. Practice the nurturing touch techniques you learned during Family Nurturing Time. You can also use the activities presented in the nurturing booklets: *Activities Manual for Infants*, *Activities Manual for Toddlers*, or *Activities Manual for Preschoolers*.

If grandparents are participating, complete the following additional tasks.

Family Home Nurturing Hour

- Teen parents respond to the following statements:

  ° The image I think this family has of me is _____ .

  ° I guess the reason you have this image of me is because _____ .

  ° The image I would like to portray is _____ .

- End the hour with a family hug.

Session 4

Before next session:

- Spend 30 minutes each day with each of your children in nurturing play time activities. Play time is a time you and your children do fun things together. Practice the nurturing touch techniques you learned during Family Nurturing Time. You can also use the activities presented in the nurturing booklets: *Activities Manual for Infants*, *Activities Manual for Toddlers*, or *Activities Manual for Preschoolers*.

- Notice an area of growth that has occurred within the last week.

- Complete the first few pages on your pregnancy and labor in the *Memories and Developmental Milestones* booklet.

(continued on next page)

Session 4 (continued)

If grandparents are participating, complete the following additional tasks.

Family Home Nurturing Hour

- Teen parents respond to the following statements:

  ° If I could change the birth of my child in any way, I would _____ .

  ° One thought about my pregnancy that I haven't shared with anyone before is _____ .

- Grandparents respond to the following statements:

  ° If I could do one thing different when your child was born, I would _____ .

  ° One thought I have about you being a parent that I haven't shared with you before is _____ .

- End the hour with a family hug.

Session 5

Before next session:

- Read the information entitled **Skill Strips**, page 6; **Ages and Stages: Development of Children**, pages 7-9; **Development Stage: Infancy, Chronological Age: Birth to One Year**, pages 10-13; **Development Stage: Toddler, Chronological Age: One Year to Three Years**, pages 14-19; and **Development Stage: Preschool, Chronological Age: Three Years to Six Years**, pages 20-23 in your Handbook.

- Pay close attention to the skills and abilities of your child(ren). Note one thing that you observed that you weren't aware of before.

- Upon task accomplishment or effort, praise your child.

- Spend 30 minutes each day with each of your children in nurturing play time activities. Play time is a time you and your children do fun things together. Practice the nurturing touch techniques you learned during Family Nurturing Time. You can also use the activities presented in the nurturing booklets: *Activities Manual for Infants, Activities Manual for Toddlers,* or *Activities Manual for Preschoolers.*

If grandparents are participating, complete the following additional tasks.

Family Home Nurturing Hour

- Have each person discuss the impact of an inappropriate demand that was placed on him/her at some point in his/her life. What was the demand? How did it feel?

- Review the information on developmental skills for your child's age. Discuss what should be expected of the child.

- End the hour with a family hug.

Session 6

Before next session:

- Read the information entitled **Baby Proofing Your House**, page 24 and **Safety Reminders By Age**, pages 28-29 in your Handbook.

- Use the worksheet entitled **Safety Checklist**, pages 25-27 in your Handbook, to modify your living environment, making the house safe for your child.

- Do something with your appearance that will help you feel better about yourself.

- Spend 30 minutes each day with each of your children in nurturing play time activities. Play time is a time you and your children do fun things together. Practice the nurturing touch techniques you learned during Family Nurturing Time. You can also use the activities presented in the nurturing booklets: *Activities Manual for Infants*, *Activities Manual for Toddlers*, or *Activities Manual for Preschoolers*.

If grandparents are participating, complete the following additional tasks.

Family Home Nurturing Hour

- Review with your parents the information discussed about baby proofing the house.

- Go through the house with the checklist and baby proof the house.

- Share a recent moment you spent with the child that made you feel proud.

- End the hour with a family hug.

Session 7

Before next session:

- Read the information entitled **Recognizing and Understanding Feelings**, pages 30-32 and **The Four Primary Feelings**, pages 33-35 in your Handbook.

- Recognize a feeling in your child and share it with him/her.

- Recognize feelings in yourself.

- Spend 30 minutes each day with each of your children in nurturing play time activities. Play time is a time you and your children do fun things together. Practice the nurturing touch techniques you learned during Family Nurturing Time. You can also use the activities presented in the nurturing booklets: *Activities Manual for Infants*, *Activities Manual for Toddlers*, or *Activities Manual for Preschoolers*.

(continued on next page)

Session 7 (continued)

If grandparents are participating, complete the following additional tasks.

Family Home Nurturing Hour

● Teen parents and grandparents take turns responding to the following statements:

   ° One feeling I have difficulty handling is _____ .
   ° When I am feeling _____, what I need from my family is _____ .

● Discuss what would happen if you told others in your family how you really felt. Would anyone care? How would your family react?

● End the hour with a family hug.

Session 8

Before next session:

● Read the information entitled **Praising Yourself and Your Children,** pages 36-38 in your Handbook.

● Praise each child twice: once for being, once for doing.

● Praise yourself twice for either being or doing.

● Spend 30 minutes each day with each of your children in nurturing play time activities. Play time is a time you and your children do fun things together. Practice the nurturing touch techniques you learned during Family Nurturing Time. You can also use the activities presented in the nurturing booklets: *Activities Manual for Infants, Activities Manual for Toddlers,* or *Activities Manual for Preschoolers.*

If grandparents are participating, complete the following additional tasks.

Family Home Nurturing Hour

● Discuss, as a family, the difficulty in using praise in recognizing others doing or being. What family roadblocks are present?

● During the hour, practice giving and receiving praise. Repeat the activity practiced during the session.

● End the hour with a family hug.

Session 9

Before next session:

● Read the information entitled **Our Self-Esteem and Self-Concept,** page 39 and **Needs of Adults, Adolescents, and Children,** page 40 in your Handbook.

● Do at least one thing to meet a need of your own. How did you feel?

● Do at least one thing to meet a need of your children. How did you think your children felt?

(continued on next page)

Session 9 (continued)

- Spend 30 minutes each day with each of your children in nurturing play time activities. Play time is a time you and your children do fun things together. Practice the nurturing touch techniques you learned during Family Nurturing Time. You can also use the activities presented in the nurturing booklets: *Activities Manual for Infants*, *Activities Manual for Toddlers*, or *Activities Manual for Preschoolers*.

If grandparents are participating, complete the following additional tasks.

Family Home Nurturing Hour

- Teen parents and grandparents take turns responding to the following statements:

  ° One need I'm trying hard to have met is _____ . This family can help me by _____ .

  ° One primary need my child/grandchild has is _____ . The way I help him/her get the need met is by _____ .

- End the hour with a family hug.

Session 10

Before next session:

- Identify one way to get a need met that can increase your positive feelings of yourself. Write it down.

- Praise each of your children once for being and once for doing before next session.

- Do one thing for yourself. What was it?

- Spend 30 minutes each day with each of your children in nurturing play time activities. Play time is a time you and your children do fun things together. Practice the nurturing touch techniques you learned during Family Nurturing Time. You can also use the activities presented in the nurturing booklets: *Activities Manual for Infants*, *Activities Manual for Toddlers*, or *Activities Manual for Preschoolers*.

If grandparents are participating, complete the following additional tasks.

Family Home Nurturing Hour

- Teen parents and grandparents take turns responding to the following statements:

  ° As a child, what was one way your parents helped you get your needs met?

  ° What is one memory you want your child/grandchild to have regarding his/her childhood needs?

- End the hour with a family hug.

Session 11

Before next session:

- Read the information entitled **I Statements and You Messages**, pages 41-44 and **Confrontation and Criticism: Sweet and Sour Music to My Ears**, pages 45-48 in your Handbook.

- Complete the worksheet entitled **The Formula for Communicating with I Statements**, page 49 in your Handbook.

- Use I statements to express feelings and thoughts without using blaming you messages twice this week.

- Practice confrontation one time.

- Spend 30 minutes each day with each of your children in nurturing play time activities. Play time is a time you and your children do fun things together. Practice the nurturing touch techniques you learned during Family Nurturing Time. You can also use the activities presented in the nurturing booklets: *Activities Manual for Infants*, *Activities Manual for Toddlers*, or *Activities Manual for Preschoolers*.

If grandparents are participating, complete the following additional tasks.

Family Home Nurturing Hour

- Teen parents and grandparents take turns responding to the following statements:

  ° One blaming you message I constantly get is _____ .

  ° One blaming you message I constantly give is _____ .

  ° One I statement I can give instead is _____ .

- End the hour with a family hug.

Session 12

Before next session:

- Read the information entitled **Helping Children With Feelings**, page 50 in your Handbook.

- Help your child handle a feeling.

- Praise your child for handling, or trying to handle, the feeling.

- Spend 30 minutes each day with each of your children in nurturing play time activities. Play time is a time you and your children do fun things together. Practice the nurturing touch techniques you learned during Family Nurturing Time. You can also use the activities presented in the nurturing booklets: *Activities Manual for Infants*, *Activities Manual for Toddlers*, or *Activities Manual for Preschoolers*.

(continued on next page)

Session 12 (continued)   If grandparents are participating, complete the following additional tasks.

Family Home Nurturing Hour

- Discuss the feelings that are the most difficult for teen parents and grandparents to handle in themselves and in their children/grandchildren.
- Identify things to do, or ways to handle the feelings, when they come up.
- End the hour with a family hug.

Session 13

Before next session:

- Read the information entitled **Personal Power**, pages 51-52 in your Handbook.
- Provide your children an opportunity to use their personal power in a positive way. What did you do?
- Use your personal power in a positive way to enhance yourself. What did you do?
- Praise each child two times for being and doing.
- Spend 30 minutes each day with each of your children in nurturing play time activities. Play time is a time you and your children do fun things together. Practice the nurturing touch techniques you learned during Family Nurturing Time. You can also use the activities presented in the nurturing booklets: *Activities Manual for Infants*, *Activities Manual for Toddlers*, or *Activities Manual for Preschoolers*.

If grandparents are participating, complete the following additional tasks.

Family Home Nurturing Hour

- Discuss how all family members can use their personal power in positive ways.
- Discuss how members are using their personal power in a negative way.
- End the hour with a family hug.

Session 14

Before next session:

- Read the information entitled **Spoiling Your Children**, pages 53-55 in your Handbook.
- Recognize a feeling your child is expressing.
- Help your child handle a feeling.
- Praise your child for expressing the feeling.

(continued on next page)

Session 14 (continued)

- Spend 30 minutes each day with each of your children in nurturing play time activities. Play time is a time you and your children do fun things together. Practice the nurturing touch techniques you learned during Family Nurturing Time. You can also use the activities presented in the nurturing booklets: *Activities Manual for Infants*, *Activities Manual for Toddlers*, or *Activities Manual for Preschoolers*.

If grandparents are participating, complete the following additional tasks.

Family Home Nurturing Hour

- Review information discussed during the session on helping children with feelings, in recognizing feelings in children, and in spoiling children.

- Teen parents and grandparents take turns responding to the following statements:

  ° The one way I am likely to spoil my child/grandchild is by _____ .

  ° What I will do instead is _____ .

- End the hour with a family hug.

Session 15

Before next session:

- Read the information entitled **Nurturing Ways to Handle Anger**, page 56 and **Reducing My Stress**, page 58 in your Handbook.

- Complete the worksheet entitled **Handling My Anger**, page 57 in your Handbook.

- Use I statements to express feelings and thoughts without using blaming you messages.

- Identify a time when you're angry and use one of the new exercises to release your anger.

- Spend 30 minutes each day with each of your children in nurturing play time activities. Play time is a time you and your children do fun things together. Practice the nurturing touch techniques you learned during Family Nurturing Time. You can also use the activities presented in the nurturing booklets: *Activities Manual for Infants*, *Activities Manual for Toddlers*, or *Activities Manual for Preschoolers*.

If grandparents are participating, complete the following additional tasks.

Family Home Nurturing Hour

- Teen parents and grandparents take turns responding to the following statements:

  ° I feel anger at home when _____ .

(continued on next page)

Session 15 (continued)

° The way I handle my anger is usually _____ .

° The way I would like to express my anger is by _____ .

● Review the ways to express anger located in the Handbook. Is there any technique which might help you express your anger more appropriately?

● End the hour with a family hug.

Session 16

Before next session:

● Read the information entitled **Why Parents Hit Their Children**, pages 59-63 in your Handbook.

● Use alternatives to express and release your anger.

● Praise your child for cooperating.

● Notice a time when you wanted to spank your child but did something else instead. Write it down.

● Spend 30 minutes each day with each of your children in nurturing play time activities. Play time is a time you and your children do fun things together. Practice the nurturing touch techniques you learned during Family Nurturing Time. You can also use the activities presented in the nurturing booklets: *Activities Manual for Infants*, *Activities Manual for Toddlers*, or *Activities Manual for Preschoolers*.

If grandparents are participating, complete the following additional tasks.

Family Home Nurturing Hour

● Teen parents and grandparents take turns responding to the following statements:

° What I learned from being hit was _____ .

° I think children should/should not be hit because _____ .

° When ___(child's name)___ is hit, I think he/she feels _____ .

° Instead of hitting, I'm going to _____ .

● End the hour with a family hug.

Session 17

Before next session:

● Read the information entitled **Discipline, Rewards, and Punishment**, pages 64-65 in your Handbook.

● List ways you currently manage your children's behavior. What punishments and rewards do you use?

● Which of these techniques do you like? Which don't you like?

● Praise each child twice.

(continued on next page)

Session 17 (continued)

- Spend 30 minutes each day with each of your children in nurturing play time activities. Play time is a time you and your children do fun things together. Practice the nurturing touch techniques you learned during Family Nurturing Time. You can also use the activities presented in the nurturing booklets: *Activities Manual for Infants*, *Activities Manual for Toddlers*, or *Activities Manual for Preschoolers*.

If grandparents are participating, complete the following additional tasks.

Family Home Nurturing Hour

- As a family, identify two ways you manage your children's behavior that you would like to change.

- As a family, identify two things you want to learn more about when it comes to managing your child's behavior.

- End the hour with a family hug.

Session 18

Before next session:

- Read the information entitled **Verbal and Physical Redirection**, pages 66-69 in your Handbook.

- Practice verbal and physical redirection at least five times.

- Praise your child for being and doing.

- Spend 30 minutes each day with each of your children in nurturing play time activities. Play time is a time you and your children do fun things together. Practice the nurturing touch techniques you learned during Family Nurturing Time. You can also use the activities presented in the nurturing booklets: *Activities Manual for Infants*, *Activities Manual for Toddlers*, or *Activities Manual for Preschoolers*.

If grandparents are participating, complete the following additional tasks.

Family Home Nurturing Hour

- Review the steps of redirection. Practice role playing the technique.

- Teen parents and grandparents take turns responding to the following statements:

  ° I think the hardest part of redirecting a child's behavior is _____ .

  ° The one benefit I see in using redirection is _____ .

- End the hour with a family hug.

Session 19

Before next session:

- Read the information entitled **Family Rules**, pages 70-71 and **Children Deserve Rewards**, page 74 in your Handbook.

(continued on next page)

Session 19 (continued)

- Review the family rules and rewards for appropriateness. Transfer the rules established on the worksheet entitled **Establishing Family Rules**, page 72 in your Handbook, to the worksheet entitled **Rules for the Family**, page 73 in your Handbook. Post these rules on the refrigerator. Start to use these rules and keep note how often you use them. Remember, you have to follow your own rules.

- Praise your children for being and doing.

- Spend 30 minutes each day with each of your children in nurturing play time activities. Play time is a time you and your children do fun things together. Practice the nurturing touch techniques you learned during Family Nurturing Time. You can also use the activities presented in the nurturing booklets: *Activities Manual for Infants*, *Activities Manual for Toddlers*, or *Activities Manual for Preschoolers*.

- Use good touch as a reward each day.

If grandparents are participating, complete the following additional tasks.

Family Home Nurturing Hour

- Review the family rules and discuss how they apply to grandparents and teen parents in the family.

- Complete work on establishing family rules. Post the rules on the refrigerator and begin to implement them.

- End the hour with a family hug.

Session 20

Before next session:

- Read the information entitled **Punishing Behavior**, pages 75-78 in your Handbook.

- Praise and use good touch each day with each of your children.

- Continue to follow the family rules.

- Practice using the alternatives to hitting that were discussed.

- Spend 30 minutes each day with each of your children in nurturing play time activities. Play time is a time you and your children do fun things together. Practice the nurturing touch techniques you learned during Family Nurturing Time. You can also use the activities presented in the nurturing booklets: *Activities Manual for Infants*, *Activities Manual for Toddlers*, or *Activities Manual for Preschoolers*.

If grandparents are participating, complete the following additional tasks.

Family Home Nurturing Hour

- Review information discussed regarding alternatives to hitting.

- Role play the use of the various forms of punishment discussed.

- End the hour with a family hug.

Session 21

Before next session:

- Continue using redirection with your children.

- Begin (continue) teaching your children proper names for all body parts.

- Praise each of your children one time for being and one time for doing.

- Spend 30 minutes each day with each of your children in nurturing play time activities. Play time is a time you and your children do fun things together. Practice the nurturing touch techniques you learned during Family Nurturing Time. You can also use the activities presented in the nurturing booklets: *Activities Manual for Infants*, *Activities Manual for Toddlers*, or *Activities Manual for Preschoolers*.

If grandparents are participating, complete the following additional tasks.

Family Home Nurturing Hour

- Discuss the words the family will use in teaching young children in the family the names of the sexual body parts and functions.

- Teen parents and grandparents take turns responding to the following statements:

  ° The messages I received as a child about sex and nudity were _____ .
  ° The attitudes I want my child/grandchild to develop are _____ .

- End the hour with a family hug.

Session 22

Before next session:

- Continue using good touch and praise.

- Follow the family rules.

- Use alternatives to hitting.

- Spend 30 minutes each day with each of your children in nurturing play time activities. Play time is a time you and your children do fun things together. Practice the nurturing touch techniques you learned during Family Nurturing Time. You can also use the activities presented in the nurturing booklets: *Activities Manual for Infants*, *Activities Manual for Toddlers*, or *Activities Manual for Preschoolers*.

If grandparents are participating, complete the following additional tasks.

Family Home Nurturing Hour

- Teen parents respond to the following:

  ° One need that I have regarding dating and love is _____ .
  ° I would like to get this need met by _____ .

(continued on next page)

Session 22 (continued)

- Grandparents respond to the following:
  - ° One way I think you can get your need to date met and still be a good parent is by _____ .
  - ° One way I can help is by _____ .
- End the hour with a family hug.

Session 23

Before next session:

- Read the information entitled **Helping Children Manage Their Behavior,** pages 79-85 in your Handbook.

- Complete the **Problem Solving and Decision Making Worksheet,** page 84 in your Handbook.

- Give your children choices in clothing or with food selection.

- Continue implementing the family rules and using rewards.

- Practice using alternatives to hitting and yelling.

- Spend 30 minutes each day with each of your children in nurturing play time activities. Play time is a time you and your children do fun things together. Practice the nurturing touch techniques you learned during Family Nurturing Time. You can also use the activities presented in the nurturing booklets: *Activities Manual for Infants, Activities Manual for Toddlers,* or *Activities Manual for Preschoolers.*

If grandparents are participating, complete the following additional tasks.

Family Home Nurturing Hour

- Review techniques for giving children choices. Role play the techniques as a family.

- End the hour with a family hug.

Session 24

Before next session:

- Read the information entitled **Facts About AIDS,** pages 86-90 in your Handbook.

- Take personal responsibility in preventing unwanted pregnancy by utilizing contraception.

- Praise your child and yourself throughout the week.

- Take time out for yourself to enjoy time with friends.

(continued on next page)

Session 24 (continued)

- Spend 30 minutes each day with each of your children in nurturing play time activities. Play time is a time you and your children do fun things together. Practice the nurturing touch techniques you learned during Family Nurturing Time. You can also use the activities presented in the nurturing booklets: *Activities Manual for Infants*, *Activities Manual for Toddlers*, or *Activities Manual for Preschoolers*.

If grandparents are participating, complete the following additional tasks.

Family Home Nurturing Hour

- During the hour, go for a walk or play a game as a family.

- End the hour with a family hug.

Session 25

Before next session:

- Notice a time when you felt your personal space was violated. When was it and how did you feel?

- Notice a time when your child's personal space was violated. What was it and who did it? How did your child feel?

- Notice a time when you honored your child's personal space. When was it?

- Praise each child once and yourself once.

- Spend 30 minutes each day with each of your children in nurturing play time activities. Play time is a time you and your children do fun things together. Practice the nurturing touch techniques you learned during Family Nurturing Time. You can also use the activities presented in the nurturing booklets: *Activities Manual for Infants*, *Activities Manual for Toddlers*, or *Activities Manual for Preschoolers*.

If grandparents are participating, complete the following additional tasks.

Family Home Nurturing Hour

- Discuss issues of control with your family. What areas of conflict still exist between teens and parents?

- Discuss any unresolved feelings and thoughts about having another pregnancy and child.

- Discuss times when family members violate each other's personal space.

- End the hour with a family hug.

Session 26

Before next session:

- Read the information entitled **Ignoring as Behavior Management**, pages 91-92 in your Handbook.

- Practice ignoring an irritating behavior. Use the steps discussed during the session.

- Continue to use techniques to empower children by giving them choices.

- Use praise twice on each child.

- Spend 30 minutes each day with each of your children in nurturing play time activities. Play time is a time you and your children do fun things together. Practice the nurturing touch techniques you learned during Family Nurturing Time. You can also use the activities presented in the nurturing booklets: *Activities Manual for Infants*, *Activities Manual for Toddlers*, or *Activities Manual for Preschoolers*.

If grandparents are participating, complete the following additional tasks.

Family Home Nurturing Hour

- Review the steps for ignoring. Decide as a family which behaviors should be ignored.

- Spend time talking about the week and how things are going.

- End the hour with a family hug.

Session 27

Before next session:

- Read the information entitled **Stimulating and Communicating**, pages 93-94 in your Handbook.

- Do one stimulating activity each day with your child.

- Practice talking to your child by describing his/her feelings during feeding time, bath time, and changing time.

- Pay attention to your child's way of communicating with you.

- Spend 30 minutes each day with each of your children in nurturing play time activities. Play time is a time you and your children do fun things together. Practice the nurturing touch techniques you learned during Family Nurturing Time. You can also use the activities presented in the nurturing booklets: *Activities Manual for Infants*, *Activities Manual for Toddlers*, or *Activities Manual for Preschoolers*.

(continued on next page)

Session 27 (continued)

If grandparents are participating, complete the following additional tasks.

Family Home Nurturing Hour

- Teen parents and grandparents take turns responding to the following statements:

  ° Two things we can do to stimulate the growth of __(child's name)__ are _____ and _____ .

  ° Discuss as a family the way __(child's name)__ communicates his/her needs.

- End the hour with a family hug.

Session 28

Before next session:

- Practice positive touch with something—enjoy touching something.

- Practice positive touch with someone—enjoy touching someone. (Remember—you are a person.)

- Touch your child(ren) in a nurturing way.

- Spend 30 minutes each day with each of your children in nurturing play time activities. Play time is a time you and your children do fun things together. Practice the nurturing touch techniques you learned during Family Nurturing Time. You can also use the activities presented in the nurturing booklets: *Activities Manual for Infants*, *Activities Manual for Toddlers*, or *Activities Manual for Preschoolers*.

If grandparents are participating, complete the following additional tasks.

Family Home Nurturing Hour

- Complete any discussion started during the home visit regarding hurting touch and scary touch experienced in childhood. Talking about pain is the only way of letting it go and moving on to experience new, nurturing touch.

- End the hour with a family hug.

Session 29

Before next session:

- Read the information entitled **Establishing Nurturing Routines**, pages 95-96 in your Handbook.

- Establish one daily routine that is nurturing to self.

- Praise each of your children one time for being and one time for doing.

(continued on next page)

Session 29 (continued)

- Spend 30 minutes each day with each of your children in nurturing play time activities. Play time is a time you and your children do fun things together. Practice the nurturing touch techniques you learned during Family Nurturing Time. You can also use the activities presented in the nurturing booklets: *Activities Manual for Infants*, *Activities Manual for Toddlers*, or *Activities Manual for Preschoolers*.

If grandparents are participating, complete the following additional tasks.

Family Home Nurturing Hour

- Review with your family the concept of nurturing routines.

- Teen parents and grandparents take turns responding to the following statements:

  ° One nurturing routine I need for myself is _____ .

  ° One nurturing routine I would like to see _(child's name)_ have is ____ .

- End the hour with a family hug.

Session 30

Before next session:

- Read the information entitled **Nurturing Diapering and Dressing Routines**, pages 97-98 in your Handbook.

- Practice implementing the nurturing diapering and dressing routine with each of your children.

- Praise yourself and your children.

- Continue utilizing your self-nurturing routine.

- Spend 30 minutes each day with each of your children in nurturing play time activities. Play time is a time you and your children do fun things together. Practice the nurturing touch techniques you learned during Family Nurturing Time. You can also use the activities presented in the nurturing booklets: *Activities Manual for Infants*, *Activities Manual for Toddlers*, or *Activities Manual for Preschoolers*.

If grandparents are participating, complete the following additional tasks.

Family Home Nurturing Hour

- Make a commitment to establish a nurturing diapering and dressing routine. Discuss what will be done.

- Role play diapering and dressing a child, or doll, utilizing nurturing skills.

- End the hour with a family hug.

Session 31

Before next session:

- Read the information entitled **Nurturing Feeding Time Routines**, pages 99-100; **Nutritious Foods for Children**, pages 101-104; and, **Tips for Cooking With Children**, page 105 in your Handbook.

- Practice implementing the nurturing feeding routine with each of your children.

- Continue implementing the nurturing routine during diapering and dressing.

- Spend 30 minutes each day with each of your children in nurturing play time activities. Play time is a time you and your children do fun things together. Practice the nurturing touch techniques you learned during Family Nurturing Time. You can also use the activities presented in the nurturing booklets: *Activities Manual for Infants, Activities Manual for Toddlers*, or *Activities Manual for Preschoolers*.

If grandparents are participating, complete the following additional tasks.

Family Home Nurturing Hour

- Role play nurturing feeding routine.

- Discuss how feeding was handled when you were a child.

- Have grandparents discuss their favorite feeding stories of you as a child.

- End the hour with a family hug.

Session 32

Before next session:

- Identify how you are feeling just prior to and after taking a chemical of choice (aspirin, alcohol, pot, speed, sedatives, etc.).

- Identify all the types of chemicals that are used regularly by your family members during the week.

- If chemicals are a problem, follow through on seeking professional help.

- Spend 30 minutes each day with each of your children in nurturing play time activities. Play time is a time you and your children do fun things together. Practice the nurturing touch techniques you learned during Family Nurturing Time. You can also use the activities presented in the nurturing booklets: *Activities Manual for Infants, Activities Manual for Toddlers*, or *Activities Manual for Preschoolers*.

(continued on next page)

Session 32 (continued)   If grandparents are participating, complete the following additional tasks.

Family Home Nurturing Hour

- Take turns responding to the following statements:
  - ° The chemical I use most often is _____ .
  - ° I use this chemical when I'm feeling _____ .
- Have all family members discuss each person's use of chemicals.
- End the hour with a family hug.

Session 33   **Before next session:**

- Spend 30 minutes each day with each of your children in nurturing play time activities. Play time is a time you and your children do fun things together. Practice the nurturing touch techniques you learned during Family Nurturing Time. You can also use the activities presented in the nurturing booklets: *Activities Manual for Infants*, *Activities Manual for Toddlers*, or *Activities Manual for Preschoolers*.
- Continue practicing nurturing routines.
- Continue utilizing alternatives to hitting.
- Recognize a time your peers wanted you to do something you didn't want to do. What happened?

If grandparents are participating, complete the following additional tasks.

Family Home Nurturing Hour

- Teen parents respond to the following:
  - ° What my friends mean to me is _____ .
  - ° Because I'm a teen parent, my friends treat me _____ .
  - ° My biggest concern regarding my friends is _____ .
- Grandparents respond to the following:
  - ° One thing about your friends that I like is _____ ;   that I don't like is _____ .
  - ° My biggest concern about your friends is _____ .
- End the hour with a family hug.

Session 34   **Before next session:**

- Read the information entitled **Nurturing Bath Time Routine**, pages 107-108 in your Handbook.

(continued on next page)

Session 34 (continued)

- Practice implementing the nurturing bath time routine with each of your children.

- Continue to practice the other nurturing routines during feeding times and diapering and dressing times.

- Praise yourself and your children.

- Spend 30 minutes each day with each of your children in nurturing play time activities. Play time is a time you and your children do fun things together. Practice the nurturing touch techniques you learned during Family Nurturing Time. You can also use the activities presented in the nurturing booklets: *Activities Manual for Infants, Activities Manual for Toddlers*, or *Activities Manual for Preschoolers*.

If grandparents are participating, complete the following additional tasks.

Family Home Nurturing Hour

- Teen parents and grandparents take turns responding to the following statements:

  ° The fondest memory I have of taking a bath as a child is _____ .

  ° The memory I want my (grand)child to have about taking a bath is _____ .

- Review the information on establishing a nurturing tubby time routine.

- End the hour with a family hug.

Session 35

Before next session:

- Read the information entitled **Nurturing Bedtime Routine**, pages 109-111 in your Handbook.

- Practice implementing the nurturing bedtime routine with each of your children.

- Continue to practice the other nurturing routines during feeding times, diapering and dressing times, and bath times.

- Spend 30 minutes each day with each of your children in nurturing play time activities. Play time is a time you and your children do fun things together. Practice the nurturing touch techniques you learned during Family Nurturing Time. You can also use the activities presented in the nurturing booklets: *Activities Manual for Infants, Activities Manual for Toddlers*, or *Activities Manual for Preschoolers*.

(continued on next page)

Session 35 (continued)

Family Home Nurturing Hour

- Teen parents and grandparents take turns responding to the following statements:

    ° One fear I have of growing older is _____ .

    ° One positive aspect of growing older is _____ .

- As a family, reveiw the information on establishing a nurturing routine for getting children to bed.

- End the hour with a family hug.

Session 36

No Home Practice Exercise this session.

Session 37

Before next session:

- Read the information entitled **Toilet Training**, pages 112-116 in your Handbook.

- If your child is old enough and capable enough, begin practicing potty training your child with the techniques and steps identified in the resource material.

- Continue to confront rather than criticize.

- Spend 30 minutes each day with each of your children in nurturing play time activities. Play time is a time you and your children do fun things together. Practice the nurturing touch techniques you learned during Family Nurturing Time. You can also use the activities presented in the nurturing booklets: *Activities Manual for Infants*, *Activities Manual for Toddlers*, or *Activities Manual for Preschoolers*.

If grandparents are participating, complete the following additional tasks.

Family Home Nurturing Hour

- Discuss how and when potty training will begin. Make sure everyone is clear on his/her role.

- Have grandparents discuss in greater detail how they potty trained you as a child.

- End the hour with a family hug.

Session 38

Before next session:

- Spend 30 minutes each day with each of your children in nurturing play time activities. Play time is a time you and your children do fun things together. Practice the nurturing touch techniques you learned during Family Nurturing Time. You can also use the activities presented in the nurturing booklets: *Activities Manual for Infants*, *Activities Manual for Toddlers*, or *Activities Manual for Preschoolers*.

- Paint or draw a picture of your relationship with your children. Have them add their feelings too!

- Practice using the nurturing routines you learned.

If grandparents are participating, complete the following additional tasks.

Family Home Nurturing Hour

- Go for a walk together and discuss how each person and the family has changed.

- End the hour with a family hug.

Session 39

Before next session:

- Spend 30 minutes each day with each of your children in nurturing play time activities. Play time is a time you and your children do fun things together. Practice the nurturing touch techniques you learned during Family Nurturing Time. You can also use the activities presented in the nurturing booklets: *Activities Manual for Infants*, *Activities Manual for Toddlers*, or *Activities Manual for Preschoolers*.

- Continue using the information and skills learned in the program with yourself and child(ren).

Session 40

Congratulations to you on a job well done!

Group-Based Home Practice Exercises

Following are Home Practice Exercises for you to complete. They will help you practice the new skills you learned during each session. Write your response on a separate sheet of paper. Do your best and share your responses with the group during the next session.

Session 1

Before next session:

- Read the information entitled **Program Orientation**, pages 1-2 and **Nurturing Program for Parents and Children**, pages 3-5 in your Handbook.

- Spend 30 minutes each day with each of your children in nurturing play time activities. Play time is a time with you and your children alone — no TV, no other distractions. Playing a game and reading books are good activities. Practice the activities listed in the *Activities Manual for Infants*, *Activities Manual for Toddlers*, or *Activities Manual for Preschoolers*. Add information to the *Memories and Developmental Milestones* booklet. Remember what you did and report next week.

Session 2

Before next session:

- Spend 30 minutes each day with each of your children in nurturing play time activities. Play time is a time you and your children do fun things together. Practice the nurturing touch techniques you learned during Family Nurturing Time. You can also use the activities presented in the nurturing booklets: *Activities Manual for Infants*, *Activities Manual for Toddlers*, or *Activities Manual for Preschoolers*.

- Do something to help yourself feel good. Share it with the group next week.

- Complete the first few pages on your pregnancy and labor in the *Memories and Developmental Milestones booklet*.

Session 3

Before next session:

- Read the information entitled **Skill Strips**, page 6; **Ages and Stages: Development of Children**, pages 7-9; **Development Stage: Infancy, Chronological Age: Birth to One Year**, pages 10-13; **Development Stage: Toddler, Chronological Age: One Year to Three Years**, pages 14-19; **Development Stage: Preschool, Chronological Age: Three Years to Six Years**, pages 20-23; **Baby Proofing Your House**, page 24 and **Safety Reminders By Age**, pages 28-29 in your Handbook.

- Use the worksheet entitled **Safety Checklist**, pages 25-27 in your Handbook, to modify your living environment, making the house safe for your child.

(continued on next page)

Session 3 (continued)	● Be aware of the expectations you place on your children. Are they appropriate for their age?
	● Spend 30 minutes each day with each of your children in nurturing play time activities. Play time is a time you and your children do fun things together. Practice the nurturing touch techniques you learned during Family Nurturing Time. You can also use the activities presented in the nurturing booklets: *Activities Manual for Infants*, *Activities Manual for Toddlers*, or *Activities Manual for Preschoolers*
Session 4	**Before next session:**
	● Read the information entitled **Recognizing and Understanding Feelings**, pages 30-32 and **The Four Primary Feelings**, pages 33-35; and **Praising Your Self and Your Children**, pages 36-38 in your Handbook.
	● Praise each child twice: once for being, once for doing.
	● Praise yourself twice for either being or doing.
	● Praise other members in your family once.
	● Spend 30 minutes each day with each of your children in nurturing play time activities. Play time is a time you and your children do fun things together. Practice the nurturing touch techniques you learned during Family Nurturing Time. You can also use the activities presented in the nurturing booklets: *Activities Manual for Infants*, *Activities Manual for Toddlers*, or *Activities Manual for Preschoolers*.
Session 5	**Before next session:**
	● Read the information entitled **Our Self-Esteem and Self-Concept**, page 39 and **Needs of Adults, Adolescents, and Children**, page 40 in your Handbook.
	● Do at least one thing to meet a need of your own. How did you feel?
	● Do at least one thing to meet a need of your children. How did you think your children felt?
	● Spend 30 minutes each day with each of your children in nurturing play time activities. Play time is a time you and your children do fun things together. Practice the nurturing touch techniques you learned during Family Nurturing Time. You can also use the activities presented in the nurturing booklets: *Activities Manual for Infants*, *Activities Manual for Toddlers*, or *Activities Manual for Preschoolers*.

Session 6

Before next session:

- Read the information entitled **I Statements and You Messages**, pages 41-44; **Confrontation and Criticism: Sweet and Sour Music to My Ears**, pages 45-48; and **Helping Children With Feelings**, page 50 in your Handbook.

- Complete the worksheet entitled **The Formula for Communicating with I Statements**, page 49 in your Handbook.

- Recognize a feeling your child is expressing by using you messages.

- Help your child handle a feeling.

- Use I statements to express feelings and thoughts without using blaming you messages twice this week.

- Spend 30 minutes each day with each of your children in nurturing play time activities. Play time is a time you and your children do fun things together. Practice the nurturing touch techniques you learned during Family Nurturing Time. You can also use the activities presented in the nurturing booklets: *Activities Manual for Infants*, *Activities Manual for Toddlers*, or *Activities Manual for Preschoolers*.

Session 7

Before next session:

- Read the information entitled **Personal Power**, pages 51-52 and **Spoiling Your Children**, pages 53-55 in your Handbook.

- Provide your children an opportunity to use their personal power in a positive way. What did you do?

- Use your personal power in a positive way to enhance yourself. What did you do?

- Praise each child two times for being and for doing.

- Spend 30 minutes each day with each of your children in nurturing play time activities. Play time is a time you and your children do fun things together. Practice the nurturing touch techniques you learned during Family Nurturing Time. You can also use the activities presented in the nurturing booklets: *Activities Manual for Infants*, *Activities Manual for Toddlers*, or *Activities Manual for Preschoolers*.

Session 8

Before next session:

- Read the information entitled **Nurturing Ways to Handle Anger**, page 56; **Reducing My Stress**, page 58; **Why Parents Hit Their Children**, pages 59-63 in your Handbook.

- Complete the worksheet entitled **Handling My Anger**, page 57 in your Handbook.

(continued on next page)

Session 8 (continued)

- Use I statements to express feelings and thoughts without using blaming you messages.

- Continue using your personal power in positive ways to meet your needs and your children's needs.

- Remember a time when you wanted to hit your children but didn't. What did you do instead?

- Spend 30 minutes each day with each of your children in nurturing play time activities. Play time is a time you and your children do fun things together. Practice the nurturing touch techniques you learned during Family Nurturing Time. You can also use the activities presented in the nurturing booklets: *Activities Manual for Infants*, *Activities Manual for Toddlers*, or *Activities Manual for Preschoolers*.

Session 9

Before next session:

- Read the information entitled **Discipline, Rewards, and Punishment**, pages 64-65 and **Verbal and Physical Redirection**, pages 66-69 in your Handbook.

- Practice verbal and physical redirection at least five times.

- Praise your child for being and doing.

- Notice a time when you wanted to spank your child but did something else instead. Write it down.

- Spend 30 minutes each day with each of your children in nurturing play time activities. Play time is a time you and your children do fun things together. Practice the nurturing touch techniques you learned during Family Nurturing Time. You can also use the activities presented in the nurturing booklets: *Activities Manual for Infants*, *Activities Manual for Toddlers*, or *Activities Manual for Preschoolers*.

Session 10

Before next session:

- Read the information entitled **Family Rules**, pages 70-71 and **Children Deserve Rewards**, page 74 in your Handbook.

- Review the family rules and rewards for appropriateness. Transfer the rules established on the worksheet entitled **Establishing Family Rules**, page 72 in your Handbook, to the worksheet entitled **Rules for the Family**, page 73 in your Handbook. Post these rules on the refrigerator. Start to use these rules and make note of how often you use them. Remember, you have to follow your own rules.

- Use your rewards each day with your children.

(continued on next page)

Session 10 (continued)

- Begin using proper names for all body parts.

- Spend 30 minutes each day with each of your children in nurturing play time activities. Play time is a time you and your children do fun things together. Practice the nurturing touch techniques you learned during Family Nurturing Time. You can also use the activities presented in the nurturing booklets: *Activities Manual for Infants, Activities Manual for Toddlers*, or *Activities Manual for Preschoolers*.

Session 11

Before next session:

- Read the information entitled **Punishing Behavior,** pages 75-78 in your Handbook.

- Continue using redirection, family rules, and rewards.

- Begin using alternatives to hitting and yelling.

- Praise each of your children each day for being and doing.

- Spend 30 minutes each day with each of your children in nurturing play time activities. Play time is a time you and your children do fun things together. Practice the nurturing touch techniques you learned during Family Nurturing Time.

Session 12

Before next session:

- Read the information entitled **Helping Children Manage Their Behavior,** pages 79-85 in your Handbook.

- Complete the worksheet entitled **Problem Solving and Decision Making Worksheet,** page 84 in your Handbook.

- Praise yourself and each of your children each day.

- Continue implementing the family rules and using rewards.

- Practice using alternatives to hitting and yelling.

- Spend 30 minutes each day with each of your children in nurturing play time activities. Play time is a time you and your children do fun things together. Practice the nurturing touch techniques you learned during Family Nurturing Time. You can also use the activities presented in the nurturing booklets: *Activities Manual for Infants, Activities Manual for Toddlers*, or *Activities Manual for Preschoolers*.

Session 13

Before next session:

- Read the information entitled **Ignoring as Behavior Management,** pages 91-92 in your Handbook.

(continued on next page)

Session 13 (continued)

- Notice a time when you felt your personal space was violated. When was it and how did you feel?

- Notice a time when your child's personal space was violated. When was it and who did it? How did your child feel?

- Notice a time when you honored your child's personal space or right to say "no."

- Practice ignoring an irritating behavior. Use the steps discussed during the session.

- Spend 30 minutes each day with each of your children in nurturing play time activities. Play time is a time you and your children do fun things together. Practice the nurturing touch techniques you learned during Family Nurturing Time. You can also use the activities presented in the nurturing booklets: *Activities Manual for Infants*, *Activities Manual for Toddlers*, or *Activities Manual for Preschoolers*.

Session 14

Before next session:

- Read the information entitled **Stimulating and Communicating**, pages 93-94 in your Handbook.

- Do one activity with your child that is stimulating.

- Practice talking to your child by describing his/her feelings during feeding time, bath time, and changing time.

- Pay attention to your child's way of communicating with you.

- Spend 30 minutes each day with each of your children in nurturing play time activities. Play time is a time you and your children do fun things together. Practice the nurturing touch techniques you learned during Family Nurturing Time. You can also use the activities presented in the nurturing booklets: *Activities Manual for Infants*, *Activities Manual for Toddlers*, or *Activities Manual for Preschoolers*.

Session 15

Before next session:

- Read the information entitled **Establishing Nurturing Routines**, pages 95-96 and **Nurturing Diapering and Dressing Routines**, pages 97-98 in your Handbook.

- Establish one daily routine that is nurturing to self.

- Praise each of your children one time for being and one time for doing.

- Spend 30 minutes each day with each of your children in nurturing play time activities. Play time is a time you and your children do fun things together. Practice the nurturing touch techniques you learned during Family Nurturing Time. You can also use the activities presented in the nurturing booklets: *Activities Manual for Infants*, *Activities Manual for Toddlers*, or *Activities Manual for Preschoolers*.

Session 16

Before next session:

- Read the information entitled **Nurturing Feeding Time Routines**, pages 99-100; **Nutritious Foods for Children**, pages 101-104; and, **Tips for Cooking With Children**, page 105 in your Handbook.

- Practice implementing the nurturing feeding routine with each of your children.

- Continue implementing the nurturing routine during diapering and dressing.

- Spend 30 minutes each day with each of your children in nurturing play time activities. Play time is a time you and your children do fun things together. Practice the nurturing touch techniques you learned during Family Nurturing Time. You can also use the activities presented in the nurturing booklets: *Activities Manual for Infants, Activities Manual for Toddlers,* or *Activities Manual for Preschoolers.*

Session 17

Before next session:

- Read the information entitled **Nurturing Bath Time Routine**, pages 107-108 in your Handbook.

- Practice implementing the nurturing bath time routine with each of your children.

- Continue to practice the other nurturing routines during feeding times and diapering and dressing times.

- Spend 30 minutes each day with each of your children in nurturing play time activities. Play time is a time you and your children do fun things together. Practice the nurturing touch techniques you learned during Family Nurturing Time. You can also use the activities presented in the nurturing booklets: *Activities Manual for Infants, Activities Manual for Toddlers,* or *Activities Manual for Preschoolers.*

Session 18

Before next session:

- Read the information entitled **Nurturing Bedtime Routine**, pages 109-111 in your Handbook.

- Practice implementing the nurturing bedtime routine with each of your children.

- Continue to practice the other nurturing routines during feeding times, diapering and dressing times, and bath times.

- Spend 30 minutes each day with each of your children in nurturing play time activities. Play time is a time you and your children do fun things together. Practice the nurturing touch techniques you learned during Family Nurturing Time. You can also use the activities presented in the nurturing booklets: *Activities Manual for Infants, Activities Manual for Toddlers,* or *Activities Manual for Preschoolers.*

Session 19

Before next session:

- Read the information entitled **Toilet Training**, pages 112-116 in your Handbook.

- If your child is old enough and capable enough, begin practicing potty training your child with the techniques and steps identified in the resource material.

- Spend 30 minutes each day with each of your children in nurturing play time activities. Play time is a time you and your children do fun things together. Practice the nurturing touch techniques you learned during Family Nurturing Time. You can also use the activities presented in the nurturing booklets: *Activities Manual for Infants*, *Activities Manual for Toddlers*, or *Activities Manual for Preschoolers*.

Session 20

Congratulations to you on a job well done!

Dear Parent:

Congratulations on completing the program. The energy you put into showing your thoughts and feelings has made you a better person. It has also helped your family interact in more pleasant ways. What you learned now needs to be put into practice throughout your lifetime. Nurturing, caring, sharing, and learning are forever, not just for a brief period. There will be times like before, that are challenging. Hang in there — don't lose your cool. Refer to the information in this Handbook or call a friend you made in the program. Don't give up. Remember change is evolutionary, not revolutionary. Keep working at being the person you want to be and the family you would like to have. Your commitment to nurturing is really just beginning.

Thanks again for your hard work. The world really is a better place because of your efforts.

Stephen J. Bavolek
Julianna Dellinger-Bavolek